T0165608

Short Strolls in
Faith

B. A. Brightlight

WestBow
PRESS
A DIVISION OF THOMAS NELSON

WestBow Press books may be ordered through booksellers or by contacting:

WestBow Press
A Division of Thomas Nelson
1663 Liberty Drive
Bloomington, IN 47403
www.westbowpress.com
1 (866) 928-1240

ISBN: 978-1-4908-1545-9 (sc)
ISBN: 978-1-4908-1546-6 (hc)
ISBN: 978-1-4908-1544-2 (e)

Library of Congress Control Number: 2013920238

Printed in the United States of America.

WestBow Press rev. date: 11/26/2013

Contents

Introduction

Let's take a walk—a short stroll along life's path—a journey in faith. This is a collection of stories from ordinary people sharing the extraordinary experience of living a life following the footsteps of our Lord Jesus Christ. The contributing authors are not preachers, Bible scholars, or theologians. They do not wear the white collar of clergy. As such, they are "blue collar" in their walk of faith—being salt and light and adding a little flavor and brightness to those around them while they pick up their lunch pail and head to their job, vocation, or "other duties as assigned." They are businessmen and women, retirees, and stay-at-home moms.

These are personal stories, poems, or a simple spiritual observation devoted to applying the wisdom of scripture to everyday life. Each story could serve as a daily devotion to the reader. The authors' objective is to share their perspective on being a blessing to others, serving and encouraging one another, and promoting the Good News of the Gospel.

The book is dedicated to the glory of God. These are turbulent times in which we live and even our nation is struggling. The future looks dark and many seem unaware or apathetic to the danger. Yet God is in control and if we join together in faith and renew our love and commitment to our Heavenly Father, then this could become America's finest hour. It would amaze ourselves and astonish the world! It's our choice and it starts within our hearts. We begin with love—for God and for others.

So get comfortable and enjoy the book, and we hope that God will inspire and fill your heart with encouragement, insight, and peace.

1. All the Wasted Time

Rick Saltzer

"So I guess I'm dying, huh?" she asked me with a tone of exhausted resignation. *Boom!* There it was—the question we had successfully avoided all day. My dad and brother had long been asleep upstairs, and it was well past 2:00 a.m. Now that we were alone and the house was completely quiet save for the ominous clicking of the oxygen machine, my mother apparently felt it was time to address the dreaded subject.

I, however, was not ready. Her frank query had caught me with my guard down; one minute, I was relaxed and reading the Bible to her, and the next, she had me pinned with the bluntest question imaginable.

Like a naughty child caught in a lie, I swallowed hard and quickly looked away. My mind raced for something soothing but substantial to say. The matter-of-fact manner in which Mom had asked the question unnerved me. It was as if she had been merely watching us and waiting for someone to have the guts to tell her what she already knew.

With much effort, I made myself look over at her on the bed, and I managed to mumble something rambling and stupid about the universal nature of death.

She said nothing; she was patiently waiting for her son to cease the pseudo-philosophy and answer her question. Her expression almost appeared to be one of pity for me in my obvious discomfort rather than concern for herself and my response. When I had gathered my thoughts and was able to spit out what the oncologist had told us earlier that morning, she remained silent, but her face took on a remarkable look of relief and serenity. Seemingly satisfied by hearing the truth, she calmly leaned back on her pillow and asked me to continue reading to her from John.

After several minutes, I glanced up and saw that she was paying virtually no attention to me. I read on until I noticed that her eyes were darting rapidly and intently around the walls of the living room where we had set up her bed. It took me a while to figure out that she was actually studying the family photographs that lined the tables and walls surrounding her.

Worried about this sudden change in her demeanor, I tried to interrupt her manic state by asking what she was thinking. Little did I know, at that point, the impact that her reply would have on my life.

Without looking at me and continuing to gaze at the familiar faces, she sighed and said, almost offhandedly, "All the wasted time…all the wasted time, and none of it even mattered."

That brief exchange turned out to be the last bit of lucid dialogue I ever had with Mom. She faded in and out of consciousness for the next three weeks or so, and died early on a hot June morning with her three guys by her side, amidst a roomful of her best memories. She had accepted Christ as her Savior a few years prior to her illness, and she was prepared and ready to move on to be with Him. All she had needed to finally let go was a confirmation that her physical fight was over and a last chance to visually drink in the most significant images of her life.

However, Mom's unabashed deathbed observation never left me. The truth that she realized and shared with me in her last moments has served as the rock of wisdom around which I have attempted to live my life ever since. Though spoken indirectly, my mother's final advice to not waste time was the best gift she ever could have given me. I was taught my most valuable life lesson by a loved one facing impending death.

Now it would be incumbent upon me to live my own life so as not to have similar regrets when God called me home.

Most Christian believers are familiar with the Bible verses that exhort us to make good use of our time: Ephesians 5:15–17; Matthew 6:19–34/ Luke 12:22–34; Luke 19:11–27; Matthew 22:36–40; and Ecclesiastes 12:8–14, for example. We study and discuss these fundamental teachings in church and Sunday school our entire Christian lives. But how often and with what degree of regularity do we apply these truths in day-to-day living?

Here are some of the questions I was forced to ask myself after that long night with my mom:

- Did I know what was truly important in life? Did I know what was temporal versus eternal?
- Did I know what truly mattered in terms of eternity? Did I truly love others?
- Did I expend too much time fretting over things and events rather than using my time to serve others?
- Did I spend too much time on amusement/entertainment? Did I find myself "killing time?"
- Did I complicate my life unnecessarily with meaningless distractions?

In a nutshell, would I discipline myself to use the time that God had given me in a manner more pleasing to Him? Would I use my time more wisely so that I'd never have to reflect bitterly upon "all the wasted time" when my life was ending? Would I use her view of the past to alter my future?

Yes, I decided. *I will.*

And that decision to reset my priorities and redirect my time changed my life forever.

Thanks, Mom.

2. Facing our Fears

Doug Hanson

It was late in September 2004 when I made my return visit to Reghin, Romania, to visit with Oana Frandes's family. I had met Oana one year earlier on a flight from Atlanta, and she had become a valuable translator for research into the whereabouts of orphans who had been displaced from the Walk in the Light orphanage and scattered across northern Romania. Her mother, Maria, was kind enough to put me up in her apartment near the town square, and she had prepared the living room couch for my bedding prior to my visit.

The next morning dawned beautifully crisp with a fresh wind down from the Ukraine and clear blue skies. Oana wanted me to see the local orphanage of twenty children, which was sponsored by a UK philanthropic organization that was also near the square. For several years, Oana had volunteered there, caring for the kids and building solid relationships with them. Following general introductions to the staff and most of the kids, Oana suggested that we paint the kids' faces using the stamping method since there were so many of them. Volunteering as the guinea pig, Oana asked for a spider, and the manager asked for a butterfly on her cheek. When they were both finished, all of the kids wanted their choices. They waited in line for almost an hour before we completed the entire group.

With this success behind us and the noon hour approaching, Oana and I moved to the central park to set up a painting site on a concrete bench. We looked for kids to paint and to bring some joy to their day. Business was slow, so Oana opted to put on a bright gold metallic wig, and she walked over to the nearby swings to round up some early volunteers. She had little trouble getting a group together, and soon I was busy painting lots of kids' faces. Each selected his or her design from some books that I had brought with me.

After six or seven kids had their entire faces painted, and they dispersed throughout the park, more and more kids became intrigued with the free offering. Oana was very patient in translating to me their preferences, and the kids and their parents delighted in the unusual opportunity.

After a few more were painted, a couple and their young son, who looked about six, slowly approached our painting venue. The young boy was crying, and the parents were busy consoling him. It turned out the boy had been sitting in a dentist's chair in a nearby third-floor office building near the park, and he had become frightened with the prospect of a tooth extraction. In Romania, dentists do not use Novocain, and children are petrified when they think about having their teeth pulled. The boy's parents had suggested a walk in the park to settle the youngster down. They saw the commotion around our face paintings and approached the area with interest.

I asked the little boy what he wanted to do. He said he wanted to scare the dentist because the dentist had scared him. "Fair enough," I said. "What would you like your face to be?" I asked. "A tigre," he replied which is Romanian for tiger.

With great confidence, the little guy brightened, straddled the concrete bench, and faced me for the white, yellow, and orange base coat. Then, after a few minutes of drying time, I painted the outline of the eyes, the nose, and the whiskers, and he was finished. When he saw his face in a hand mirror, he exclaimed, "Let's go!" His confidence had returned, and he was ready to scare his dentist.

At least forty minutes passed as numerous other boys and girls came for their personal makeovers. Laughter and joy abounded as the kids looked at one another and enjoyed the moment. Oana gave them instructions for washing off the paint later in the day, and excitedly, the kids kept scouting for more of their friends to join in their fun.

It was then that I looked down the long, pebbled path to see one of my painted faces approaching our area. It was the little guy coming from his successful dental appointment holding the hands of both his parents. He had told his parents that he wanted to return to me to give me a hug and thank me for giving him this new courage to frighten his dentist and endure the pain of the extraction.

I was almost in tears as I hugged the little guy. I took a moment to contemplate the situation: Here I was halfway around the world in a country where I did not know the language providing a bit of fun and entertainment that few of these children had ever experienced. I had no signs for advertising and took no pay for services. I was there in Reghin for this one little guy who, without his tiger "face" of courage, would have had a frightening experience in the dental chair. It was a moment in time orchestrated by God to use me in a most unexpected way to make a difference in this little man's day, and perhaps in his life, along with many others who braved their fears to approach this American visitor.

Oana could not contain her joy as we left the park after spending three hours with the kids. It was a day she too would never forget.

3. Lost

Tom McAllister

Have you ever been lost—or worse, lost and alone? I'm not talking about being unable to find someone's house or a restaurant when you're just a few blocks away and too stubborn to stop and ask directions. (Pride can be *such* an impediment to success.) No, I'm referring to a situation where you don't have a clue as to where you are or whether the direction you are currently traveling in is any improvement upon your predicament. It's not a good feeling, is it?

I once got lost as a small child while our family was camping in Florida. It was not an excellent adventure. Through retrospective rationalization, I've determined that it was really my sister's fault. Knowing how to place blame is a valuable skill set—at least in our own minds.

When I was growing up, our family did a lot of camping. Mom and Dad would load up us kids in our camper and take us somewhere, and in this case, it was Florida. We were in a large campground with hundreds of campers, RVs, and trailers. A trading post stood near the center of the campground. One night, my older sister and I walked to this general store, and I saw some Batman cards. Like most six-year-olds, I wanted them. Now these weren't the *Dark Knight* Batman cards of today. These were the more cartoonish Batman and Robin, who fought bad guys with the *"POW,"* *"WHAM,"* and *"ZOWEE"* type of thing—more appropriate for a small youngster. My sister kept teasing me that she was not going to buy them for me.

All of you "babies" of the family out there know that it's a tough life being the youngest. So like any respectable, rebellious, recent graduate of kindergarten who was determined to get what he wanted, I ran out of the store to find my mom or dad and plead my case up the chain of command.

And I got lost.

I wandered up and down several roads for a few hours in the dark, crying and totally confused as to where I was. My parents, along with a few camping neighbors, set out to find me. Mom was worried that I might get run over by a car or bitten by a snake. One of the fellow campers said that this probably wouldn't happen, but two dogs had gone missing over the past week, and they thought an alligator had gotten them. (There's nothing like positive words of encouragement to help alleviate the stress of a worried mother.)

Finally, a fellow camper found me and took me to my family's campsite. My parents were greatly relieved to find me. Then, once I was safe, the judgment came. That was the only time my dad took off his belt and gave me a whipping. To complete this endearing father-son moment, my dad even told me that old cliché, "Son, this is going to hurt me more than it does you."

I sobbed in response, "Then why aren't you crying?" You know, sometimes it is best in situations like that just to be quiet and take your licking. Later, my sister did buy me the Batman cards. Somehow, they had lost their luster and appeal after that ordeal—a negative return-on-investment as the gain was well below the cost.

Despite that traumatic experience, being physically lost pales in comparison to being spiritually lost. In fact, there is no comparison—none whatsoever. There is no more appropriate use of the warning, "DON'T GO THERE!"

Ponder the following logical reasoning for a moment:

- ❧ If there is a Creator of the universe (God), and…
- ❧ if this Creator has established for humanity a life after this earthly one that has far greater potential in terms of duration (i.e. eternity) and fulfillment (i.e. joy/peace/paradise) than this life, and…
- ❧ if what you say, think, do, and believe in this life somehow affects the outcome or the status of your next life, then…
- ❧ "How should you live your life?"

Well, holy perpetuity pontification, Batman! Is this the ultimate riddle from the Riddler for us to consider?

Let's break this down in terms of return on investment (ROI). If there exists a future life after this earthly life that just knocks the socks slap off your feet, and it, like the Energizer Bunny, keeps going and going in a perfectly pleasing and particularly pleasurable manner, then how can you even quantify love, joy, and peace for all eternity? It goes right off the chart.

This truly is a no-brainer (but keep your brain, as you will need it to read further). The simple answer is to say, think, do, and believe whatever it is that pleases the Creator. He's the One giving out the brownie points. *Duh.* Your payback is incalculable. Think about it. Even in the worst possible scenario for this earthly life, this is still an awesome deal.

Let's consider the worst-case scenario. Here's an analogy. Perhaps you've seen the television show *Dirty Jobs*. It portrays all sorts of undesirable occupations from the slightly unappealing to the grotesquely nasty. Let's say you've become a contestant who has to perform the worst possible job in the world; dream up your worst. You must work this job for an entire month. To make the job even more miserable, your living conditions during that month will be equivalent to those experienced by the poorest of the poor.

After that one month, however, you get to retire in a mansion on a wonderful beach where you will live in luxury for the rest of your life. Would you take on such a challenge? What if how hard you worked during that month determined your benefits and privileges in retirement? Would you work your hardest? Of course, you would—or you should. What's one month compared to the rest of your life? In the grander, real-life scheme, what's a lifetime, even if you live to be two hundred years old, compared to two trillion years? It's less than a rounding error.

Think about this now. The eventual prize is a pleasant, pain-free life of love, peace, and joy forever. Is there any scenario in this earthly life so great or too severe that would cause us to reject this incredible offer? I can't come up with anything. Can you?

Well, that's the deal. Our Heavenly Father has promised us a life with Him for all eternity. It is a place with many mansions, and there is no pain, no suffering, and no tears except perhaps tears of joy and amazement at His abounding grace. God is love (1 John 4:8), and His love surpasses human understanding. Think about a time when you were in love and felt love from another—that "feet not touching the ground" type of love—the kind of love that fills your heart to near bursting capacity. That is so miniscule compared to the love you will receive in Heaven that it doesn't even register on the scale. If all seven billion people on Planet Earth simultaneously loved you with all their hearts, this would not come close to the immeasurable love our Heavenly Father has for you. Imagine being in an environment where you are totally immersed in such love all the time—forever! This is the plan for God's children—those whose names are written in the Book of Life. What a deal! It would require surgery to remove the smiles from our faces. In fact, it will be so wonderful that we will probably just childishly giggle with glee through the first ten thousand years.

So where do you sign up? All you must do is believe in the name of Christ Jesus and accept Him as your Lord and Savior. That's it.

In essence, it is that simple, but do not think this is some flippant, superficial notion. This is the most critical decision that you will ever make. Of all the millions of decisions we will make in a human lifetime, this one *is* the most important. In fact, it is more important than all the rest put together! It is the gateway to eternal life.

Thus being the cosmic Checkpoint Charlie and the narrow gate through which the spiritually lost gain everlasting life, we should definitely explore this further. The crux of the matter centers upon the definition of what it means to "believe" and subsequently, how one accepts Jesus Christ as Lord and Savior. What are its requirements of us?

Much analysis, thought, and prayer by very wise and devout followers of Christ has gone into this topic over the centuries to discern the details, identify the critical elements, and ascribe their level of importance to develop doctrines of the what, how, and whys of the scripturally defined concept of belief. Unfortunately, there also have arisen a lot of complicated answers and explanations to these questions, which I'll try to avoid in my explanation.

In the original Greek language, the words translated as *believe* also mean to trust, to have faith in, and to make a commitment to. Other synonyms are *to receive* and *to accept*. When you believe, there is a professing of perceived knowledge or understanding, and this knowledge and understanding has both an object and a context. The object may be a person, place, or thing, and the context is a statement about the object. Statements such as "I believe that vitamins improve my health," or "I believe the Bermuda Triangle is haunted" show an object (vitamins/the Bermuda Triangle) and the context (improve health/is haunted). This is where the English language definition of the word "believe" typically stops, as it implies just an intellectual acceptance. Notice the Greek words for believe also include the concepts of trusting and commitment. This requires going a couple of steps past mere intellectual acceptance. This knowledge and understanding is then evaluated to create an affection and desire which then develops a motivation and a will to act.

UNDERSTANDING → DESIRE → MOTIVATION

This is what it means biblically to "believe." The act of belief goes beyond intellectual acceptance to create a desire that compels one to act. Thus, in this specific instance, the object of our faith or belief is Jesus Christ. The context is that He is the Son of God, which makes Him our Lord, and His death on the cross paid the penalty for all of our sins, which makes Him our Savior. This knowledge and understanding must create an affection or desire to be considered belief. It is too fantastic a revelation to be received with apathy. *Jesus is the Son of God? Oh, how nice. Hey, did you see the game last night?* No way—this is too big a deal! If you truly believe Jesus is the Son of God Who died for you, then this will evoke a strong response in you to move toward or away from Him. This is the third step of belief: the creation of motive or an act of the will that directs our response and drives our actions.

In many respects, detailed study of this "belief" process has caused as much confusion as it has clarity. Some theologians promote a required batting order that you must first accept Jesus as Lord before He can become your Savior. Others have pursued a quantitative analysis approach to ascertain the necessary amount of understanding, the minimum threshold level of desire, and the required motivation to act, or reversing the latter by examining your acts (or lack of them) to determine if your motivation is sufficient. Though driven by good intentions, this methodology of analysis has caused much angst and dissention. There is a better and simpler way to grasp this. The debate on the what, how, how much, and whys of our belief is far less important than the Who.

As an illustration, I'll share another story from my youth—my second toddler tale of terror. In this particular story of childhood misbehavior (I seem to have several to choose from), the event occurred at the family home. Some of the details are vague, and I cannot recall what specific act of disobedience I performed to provoke my mother's wrath, but it was of sufficient seriousness to warrant immediate judgment and punishment.

Now Mom's tool of choice in those infrequent circumstances requiring justice through corporal punishment was the flyswatter, and it was strategically placed atop the refrigerator for prompt retrieval. It was "death from above" for flies, but for meting out discipline, it caused no physical harm to the punished child. It did, however, significantly reduce pride while simultaneously increasing humility and respect for authority in the offending toddler. When used for its primary purpose of swatting the occasional fly in the house, it posed no human threat, but when Mom reached for it while you were fully aware of your guilt, it was an instrument to be feared. In this particular instance, no annoying flies had entered the interior homestead airspace, but she was going for the flyswatter. *Uh-oh! Warning! Alert! Danger! Danger!* Faced with a larger aggressor (she was much bigger than I was) with advanced weaponry (the flyswatter) and superior moral authority (she was all-powerful Mom, and I was in the wrong), the primordial "fight or flight" instinct of my little brain quickly assessed the situation.

And I ran.

Oh, yes, did I run. Fueled by the adrenaline of fear, out the back door I fled with my mom in hot pursuit. It just so happened that my grandparents were in town visiting, and my grandmother, who we called Nanny, was standing out in the back yard. Spying her in my panicked state, I ran in her direction shouting and pleading with all my heart, "Save me, Nanny! Save me!"

I don't remember how that story ended and whether Nanny did "save" me or intervene on my behalf. Probably Mom had her typical compassion and mercy and commuted the punishment or at least reduced it to a verbal scolding. In this *Flee the Flyswatter* parable, I wasn't doing a lot of salvation analysis, nor did I even know if Nanny would save me, but there was a frantic hope and a completely heartfelt plea. However, I do know how it will end when we run to Jesus Christ. When we fully realize how much we need a savior, we should run in our desperation to Him shouting in earnest, "Save me, Jesus! Save me!" There is no one more loving, more willing, and more patiently waiting with outstretched arms than our Lord. He will never refuse your request.

It is this pure, heartfelt belief—this commitment of ourselves in the pure act of trust and dependence on Jesus Christ—that brings us into an eternal, loving relationship with our heavenly Father. It is not a bunch of formulas, a set of rituals and sayings, or the achievement of some intellectual insight on divine doctrine. It is a personal one-on-one encounter with the Son of God and the placement of our complete trust in Him. As you grow and mature spiritually, you will gain greater understanding of the precepts of God's loving grace, Christ's perfect sacrifice, repentance, being born again, justification, sanctification, spiritual atonement, and how to walk in faith. Learning the what, how, and why of Christianity will add depth and understanding to your faith, but it is the Who—it is Jesus Christ that is the key. All Christians agree on the Who, and *that* is the critical component. We can even strip away all reason. It simply starts with our trusting belief in Christ Jesus. Just go to Him, *run* to Him with your heart, for He is the *only* One Who can save you.

This is the Good News! This is the Gospel—the new birth and the dramatic start that will change the way we live our lives in all that we say, think, do, and believe. It is transformational—you become a new you. Some have a memorable conversion experience while for others it is like a seed planted in the ground where it takes some time before anyone (including the individual) notices a difference.

Now the benefit of accepting Jesus Christ as your Lord and Savior is much more than just an awesome ROI in the afterlife, although that alone makes it the overwhelmingly best option. It starts a new journey in your life—a personal journey of companionship with the Creator! Can you find a better tour guide to travel with you through life? You get to go with the One who created the whole universe. He designed it, drew

16

up the blueprints, and then built it, and He knows how it operates best. He has the perfect game plan, and He loves you so much that He *died* for you. He wants you to be joyful and fulfilled every day of your life. He has a perfect plan flawlessly tailored for everyone on the planet. Not only is this the best deal in town; it's the best deal in the universe! We should be shouting in the streets about it and telling everyone we know. Think about that. This is the cure for the spiritual cancer inside of every human being. This is the only antidote that works because it gives everlasting life! Should we keep this quiet as our little secret? No! We should be jumping for joy and sharing this Good News with everyone we meet!

Now there is a flip side to this Good News. It's not a catch, and it's not written in small print—the print's the same size throughout the Bible. You can choose to reject this deal of a lifetime, and if you do, you're toast—burnt toast.

This is not a joking matter—it is Bad News! This is the most awful thing you could ever imagine. Think of a time when you were in pain—*severe*, physical pain. Consider a time of mental anguish when you were very anxious, fearful and felt completely hopeless about a situation. Now magnify both of those several thousand times into a constant, continuous state of suffering. That's a gruesome thought, isn't it? But here's the real kicker. However bad that is, and it's real bad, the killer is that there is no hope of it improving—ever. It is hopeless suffering for all eternity: the complete absence of hope. It is the darkest of the dark, the worst of the worst, and more horrible than anything you can conceive. You are lost—forever.

God provides us a simple choice to make. We can be with Him or without Him, and the consequences of our decision are beyond words. Nothing on Planet Earth is even remotely enticing enough for us to choose to be without Him. Even the best possible outcome without Christ is still a total loss. Jesus presented that ROI scenario quite plainly:

"For what does it profit a man to gain the whole world, and forfeit his soul?" (Mark 8:36 NASB).

So, dear reader, it's *your* choice, and it is the most important decision you will ever make. Don't be the ultimate loser. Get on the winning team, and get in on the journey of a lifetime—the most excellent adventure of walking with His Excellency—Jesus Christ.

4. Who Dat?

Tom McAllister

Say, who dat? Who dat, who? Who dat messin' with de mighty, mighty devils?

That was one of the cheers for our high school basketball team, along with, "You fouled, my man. Hey boy, what's wrong with your head?" Perhaps in this stifling age of political correctness, such cheers would be considered inappropriate. But our team, the mighty, mighty Red Devils of Graham High School in Graham, North Carolina, went undefeated that year in 1976 and won the state 3A basketball championship.

You can't knock perfection. In the end, every 3A school in the state knew who we were.

Sometimes it's important to know who someone is, and it's always important to know who you are. If you don't know who you are, there are shelves upon shelves of books written to help you find yourself, find your inner self, discover things about yourself, love yourself, and maximize your potential. In fact, someone somewhere has written something about almost anything you've wanted to know about yourself but have been too afraid to ask.

Going back to our mighty, mighty Red Devils high school, a mural was painted on one of the cafeteria walls with the proclamation that you are what you eat. Judging by some of the food served there, as in many school cafeterias, that was a scary thought.

Although food plays an important role in our physical growth, a more encompassing assertion is to state that you are the sum total of the decisions that you make. That's an accurate statement, isn't it? You are where you are today because of the decisions you've made along the way: what car to drive, what house to buy, what food to eat, what job to take, what principles to follow, what precepts to believe, and what person to marry. *Voila. Vous etes ici.* (And now you are here).

Pastor Andy Stanley of North Point Community Church in Atlanta, Georgia, wrote an insightful book about this concept entitled, *The Principle of the Path.* Where you end up in large part is due to the cumulative decisions you make along the way. Yes, sometimes events occur well outside our control that dramatically affect our lives, but the greatest influence of why you are where you are is determined by the decisions you have made. Your intentions mattered not, as the adage states that even the road to hell is paved with good intentions. It's your steps that matter, and it is best in this journey through life that we be wise in how we take our steps.

Though we are the cumulative sum of the choices we make, the vast majority of these decisions have negligible effect on where we are in life. Pondering what flavored gum to buy or what section of the newspaper to read first rarely alters the course of human history. There are, however, a few choices and one decision in particular that have a huge impact on who we become and where we end up.

Mark records in his gospel (8:27–29 ESV) a conversation that occurred while Jesus was traveling with His disciples to villages around Caesarea Philippi. (The story is also told in Matthew 16:13 and Luke 9:18.) While they are strolling along, Jesus, perhaps casually, asks His disciples, "Who do people say that I am?"

They answer Him: "John the Baptist; and others say Elijah; but others, one of the prophets."

Then, I envision Jesus just stopping right there in the middle of the road for a dramatic pause as His disciples gather around Him. They know He is about to say something important. Slowly scanning their faces and looking intently into their eyes, Jesus asks them, "But who do you say that I am?"

This question, folks, is a biggie. And it's not just meant for the disciples; it is for every human being on the planet.

Your answer and the subsequent actions inspired by your answer is more important than what house you buy, what career you have, or what person you marry. This has eternal consequences: forever-and-ever-type stuff.

So let's pause for a moment to consider it very carefully. What's the real deal with this Jewish carpenter who lived in Palestine two thousand years ago?

First of all, no matter what you believe, you must objectively admit that no person in human history has had a greater impact on humankind than Jesus of Nazareth. Who even comes close? Here is a man who the entire world bases its calendar by the estimated date of His birth. He performed incredible miracles, taught an amazing philosophy and approach to living a life with abundance, and after being crucified, He rose from the dead! Jewish prophets predicted all these events—some over one thousand years before they were fulfilled. Peter Stoner, who is Professor Emeritus of Science at Westmont College, along with six hundred of his students, calculated the probability of one person fulfilling just eight of the biblical prophecies found in Micah 5:2, Malachi 3:1, Zechariah 9:9, Zechariah 13:6, Zechariah 11:2, Zechariah 11:13, Isaiah 53:7, and Psalm 22:16. It came out to one in one hundred thousand trillion.[1] Most Bibles list over forty prophecies fulfilled by Jesus, and some scholars claim the number of prophecies fulfilled by Christ exceed four hundred! I think the mathematics indicate that we can say with a high degree of confidence that we have our man. Today, nearly a third of the entire world considers Him to be the Son of God, and well, He either is, or he is not. It's one of those decisions that you can't be ambivalent about or simply take a pass.

Though other religions may refer to Jesus as a holy man, a prophet, a miracle worker, or a human who achieved some New Age, godlike qualities, this is wholly inadequate to what He claimed. It's worse than referring to the president of the United States as just another civil servant. Jesus claimed to be the Son of God: "I and the Father are One" (John 10:30), "Before Abraham was, I AM" (John 8:58), "I am the living bread that came down from Heaven" (John 6:51), "If you've seen Me, you've seen the Father" (John 14:9), to name just a few examples. To put it quite bluntly, either He is telling the truth or he is telling a lie. It's the ultimate *Ripley's Believe It or Not*. There is no in-between.

There are only three possibilities for Jesus—one of three Ls. He is either a liar by claiming to be the Son of God when he is not, a lunatic in that he thought he was the Son of God, but was mistaken, or He is the legitimate Son of God Who sits at the right hand of the Father and will someday come to judge the living and the dead.

Once again, this logic goes against political correctness, as truth typically does. The only way that Jesus could be a holy man, a prophet, or a good teacher is if He truly is the Son of God. For a holy man, a prophet, or a good teacher cannot lie, nor can he be insane. A legitimate prophet can only speak the truth. Jesus claimed to be the Son of God, so in order for Him to be a holy man or a prophet, He must be telling the truth. This then elevates Him above simply being a holy man or a prophet to His rightful place as the Son of God sitting at the right hand of the Father. It is this belief that Jesus is the Christ, the Messiah, and the Son of God upon which the entire Christian faith hangs. This faith is either completely right or completely wrong; there's no partial credit or consolation prize for playing.

Considering all the facts, it is difficult to imagine how anyone could conclude that Jesus Christ is a lunatic or a liar. To think such is foul: *Hey boy, what's wrong with your head?* No one would willingly go through scourging and the horrific torture of crucifixion to promote a lie. A crazy man could not speak such wisdom and perform such miracles. God would not honor a fool by allowing him to be resurrected from the dead.

Just examine the subsequent actions of the disciples. They ran in fear when Jesus was captured. Then, after seeing the resurrected Lord, they boldly went forth proclaiming the Gospel message that Jesus Christ is Lord and the Savior of the world. For these actions and many more recorded in the book of Acts, most of them were martyred. They lived beyond faith—they lived in fact as firsthand witnesses of the risen Lord. They all experienced personally the response given by Thomas, who doubted Jesus's resurrection until he could put his finger directly in the nail holes in Jesus's hands and his hand in the wound in Jesus's side. When he did this, there was only one reply possible: "My Lord and my God" (John 20:28 NASB).

What's interesting to note is the dialogue between Jesus and Thomas during this special encounter. Jesus did not admonish Thomas for his lack of faith. He didn't smack him on top of the head and say, "Whatsamatter with you? I've been with you for three years. Didn't you listen to what I was saying?" No, Jesus simply responded, "Because you have seen Me, you have believed; blessed are those who have not seen and yet have believed" (John 20:29 NASB).

Jesus did not criticize Thomas for his doubt. He did however pronounce a blessing to all those who come to Christ in faith, especially to those who arrive there without the unique privilege that Thomas had of seeing Christ for himself.

So where are you in your assessment of Jesus Christ? Are you full of doubt? Is He a liar, a lunatic, or Lord of your life? If you're still unsure, just ask Him. Jesus is not troubled by your doubt and fears. Earnestly seek Him. Call to Him with true sincerity in prayer and ask Him to reveal Himself to you. He is already knocking on the door of your heart. Ask Him to come on in.

When you do, your life will change forever. You will know who

Jesus is, and you will agree that there is only one correct answer when He asked, "But who do you say that I am?"

Peter gave the right answer when he said, "You are the Christ, the Son of the living God" (Matt. 16:16 NASB).

Don't be messing with dat devil. Get in on the winning team with God's Son. He is "our Lord and our God," and you can take that truth to the spiritual bank. Believe on it, and be saved.

5. Second Chance

Chance Castleberry

My desire is that this brings God glory and helps others see that He can save anyone and turn his or her life around.

Here is my testimony...

I was born into a broken marriage. My father was an abusive alcoholic, and my mother was addicted to gambling. They were divorced when I was a baby. My mother then remarried for the third time. I had one older brother who had cerebral palsy and was almost blind. Our lives involved continuous moving from one place to the next. This occurred every few months and sometimes every few weeks. My school records would rarely catch up with the school I was in before we moved again.

My mother was not a mean person. She was just very self-centered and desperately depressed from continual gambling and her attraction to the occult. Her life was a daily routine of going to tarot card readers and doing whatever was necessary to get cash to gamble with. Both addictions completely controlled her. As a by-product of her way of life, my brother and I were either alone most of the time or with any family member or friend she could talk into keeping us. Many times we were resented or abused because mother would promise whomever she could talk into watching us that she was to return in a few hours. But this often led to days on end without her coming back.

My brother was unusually strong emotionally, and he dealt with our life's blows with great calmness. I dealt with difficulty very poorly and craved escape—however I could find it. Life was intolerable for me until I discovered that alcohol and drugs provided instant relief from my hurt and pain. Both were readily available because most of my mother's companions were heavy drinkers, and some used drugs as well. I tried marijuana for the first time when I was nine years old. I was hopelessly addicted to drugs and alcohol by the age of twelve. Now my own demons led me to do whatever was necessary to feed my habit. By the time I turned thirteen, I was robbing houses and stealing whatever I could find to stay high. During this time, my mother placed my brother in a school for blind and disabled children. He hated it so much that he would cry and beg not to go back each time he came home for the occasional weekend. Being crippled and partially blind, he endured a hell of his own for many years. The abuse he suffered there was unspeakable and altered him permanently in many ways. With him not being around much anymore, I spiraled deeper and deeper into self-destruction and sin.

The only stability I ever knew was when I visited my grandparents on my father's side. The downside was that I had to tolerate my father when he was there. It's not that he was downright mean very often; he was just usually drunk and totally self-absorbed. I never received a single birthday or Christmas card from him. He never came to visit me my entire life. He never called me—not one single time.

But my grandparents were totally different. They were the only Christians I had ever known or been exposed to. I didn't understand what that meant at the time; I just knew that I couldn't smoke or drink when I was at their home, and I had to watch my language.

My grandfather was a jewel of a man. I always knew that he loved me unconditionally. He worked twelve-hour days and would still drive two and a half hours to pick me up every Friday evening. Then on Sunday night, he would take me back to wherever I lived at the time. I wanted to be just like him. He was honest and friendly, and when he made you a promise, you could take it to the bank. He was my absolute hero. Never has anyone shown me the kind of love that he gave me freely.

One of my mother's husbands was in the Navy, and they moved us to California when he was transferred to a base there. When I called my father to tell him that I was moving to California, he cursed me out and said I would never see him again. I tried not to disappoint him, but I never called him again, and I did not see him at all for over three years.

By this point in my life, I was getting arrested for my criminal behavior. By my third attempt at passing the eighth grade, I had changed schools eighteen times. I was always the new kid. By the time I had fought the bullies and gotten to know a few people, I was moving again. Often I did not know we were moving until I came home and saw that the car was packed and my mother was standing there saying, "Get in; we're out of here."

We moved all over Georgia, Alabama, and twice to California and back. Mother was married and divorced eight times, not to mention countless live-in boyfriends. A few were good providers, but Mother always cleaned out the bank account to gamble, and she always lost money, so she could never pay the bills. The marriages never lasted long.

At about fifteen years of age, I started at yet another school for the final time. We had been there for a couple of months, and I really liked a girl who lived nearby. I came home from school one day and saw that, once again, the car was packed. Mother was mad, and she told me that we were moving.

I completely lost it. I cursed and screamed at her until I could no longer produce sound. I said, "I will never go to school again." That's one promise I kept. Soon after that, I left my mother for good and drifted among distant relatives and various friends for years. Getting arrested was now a regular occurrence for me. The only place I ever felt at home was when I lived at my grandparents' house from time to time.

When I say I was addicted to drugs, I mean it. A typical day for me meant drinking a case or more of beer, smoking marijuana all day, and popping pain pills as well. Those were the everyday staples. I also drank hard liquor and did cocaine, speed, and LSD. You name it, and I did it any time I could get my hands on it. I got into all of the "designer drugs" that came and went as well. When I discovered who was dealing drugs, I broke into their houses and robbed them when I was desperate enough. When no drugs could be obtained, I would drink heavily and inhale lighter fluid to get high.

I could not stand being alive without drugs. I would go for weeks on end with no memory at all of the time. I drove in a total blackout more often than not. I would always fight or take off whenever the police attempted to catch me. I caused five different hit-and-run accidents. When I would get out of jail, I would party to celebrate.

In 1993, my father committed suicide on his fifty-third birthday. It didn't affect me the way you might imagine it would. I absolutely hated him and could not have cried if I had wanted to, but I felt a great sense of loss that I didn't understand. It was almost as though I mourned the father-son relationship that I had never experienced, wished I could have had, and knew for certain that I would never enjoy now.

My grandparents were absolutely devastated. My father was their only son, and now they put that mantle on me. Even though I was a total wreck, they loved me more than ever. I loved them too, but I was so selfish and lost that I had no empathy for anyone—not even them. I moved back in with my grandparents, though, and pretended to take care of them.

I brought total hell and destruction into their lives. They were somewhat wealthy, and I stole from them continually. I hated myself for it, but that didn't stop me. I became their power of attorney and spent tens of thousands of their hard-earned dollars on booze, drugs, and living the high life. They also paid the many attorneys and fines it took to keep me out of prison. Both they and everyone else knew I was worthless, but they kept on loving me, and they prayed that I would turn my life around.

My grandmother passed after a terrible few years of Alzheimer's disease. Now it was just my grandfather and me. His remaining family and friends hated me, and with good reason; they knew that I was bad news. I had total control over my grandfather's estate now, and I was a violent, vile, and dangerous individual. Sin was still my master, and I crossed all lines. I would become terribly aggressive if even questioned about my behavior, and I took it out on everyone.

Then it happened.

One night, as on so many others, I left to go barhopping in Atlanta, stoned out of my mind. Like so many times before, I couldn't remember returning home. I awoke the next morning bleeding from cuts all over my body, and my bedroom was a wreck. I knew that something bad had happened, and this was confirmed when I left my room and went downstairs. Everything in the entire house was broken, knocked over, or destroyed. At this point, I thought someone must have broken in and tried to kill us.

Then I thought about Grandpa.

I ran to search for him. When I found him, he was sitting downstairs in the only chair in the kitchen that was upright. He was crying; he had a terrible black eye, and his glasses were broken. He was also cut and bruised in several places.

I said, "Oh, my God! Who did this, Grandpa?"

I fell to my knees when he said, "You did, Son."

I had somehow always justified my rage and anger throughout my entire life, but not this time. I wet a rag and tried to clean his wounds. He was shaking, and was obviously scared of me. I was praying out loud "No, God! No!" I started crying as never before in unimaginable regret, telling him how sorry I was. I could not bear the realization of what I had done to the only one who had never wronged me. I took a knife from the kitchen and slit both of my own wrists deeply, then sat down to die.

To my shock, the police and paramedics arrived within minutes. Two amazing things happened in the middle of all of this. Neither my grandfather nor I had gotten up and called 911. Then as they were loading Grandfather into one ambulance and me into another, a kind-faced paramedic leaned down to me as if he knew me and said, "Don't worry, Chance. Your grandfather and you will be just fine. God knows you did not mean for this to happen, and we are praying for you both."

I never saw him again.

Later, we learned that the 911 call had come from our phone, but the phone had been torn off of the wall the night before.

I still thank God because my grandfather's wounds were all superficial, and he healed rapidly in the hospital. I was taken from the hospital to Laurelwood, and after several days of recovery while on suicide watch, I was taken to jail for my last time.

I had been incarcerated countless times, but this time was different. I could not deal with what I had done. I was so racked with guilt and grief that I could not get up from my metal bunk to get my food tray. I had no desire to live at all. I could see no way whatsoever to fix all that I had done, and I just kept wishing when I woke up each day that it had all been a bad dream. Jail wasn't what bothered me, nor my drug and alcohol use, nor even all the evil I had committed throughout my life—it was what I had done to my grandfather.

After many weeks had passed without any hope to carry on, an unusual and miraculous thing happened to me. I prayed that God would just please remove the hurt from my grandfather's heart and give him joy in the last years of his life. I had prayed before, but for the first time in my life, it was an unselfish prayer.

Even still, I didn't think I could be forgiven or ever have a life. I knew I was guilty, and I deserved the worst from both God and man. But suddenly, and without warning, a peace that surpassed all understanding flooded my soul! I felt God's presence, and His unconditional love enveloped me completely. It was the most beautiful thing I had ever experienced.

Suddenly, I knew forgiveness was there for me, and I asked for it. And when I did, I was totally forgiven of every sin I had ever committed by the very God who had created me! In that moment, I told the LORD that if He would set things right in my life, I would never use drugs or alcohol again. And then I would do everything I could to live a life that was pleasing to Him. I meant it.

The next day, I was still in jail. I had still hurt my grandfather, and I would still have to face the courts for what I had done. My circumstances had not changed at all, but *I* sure had! I spent the rest of my sentence in jail with humble joy. I often grieved terribly for what I had done to my grandfather, but when I did, I remembered the paramedic who had called me by name and said, "Your grandfather and you will be just fine. We are praying for you."

After my release from custody, it took me several more months to face my grandfather. I would have understood if he had rejected me forever, but I prayed for him every day and asked for his comfort. His other family members had a restraining order against me, and they still thought I was bad news. I understood this as well. I had viciously hurt the one man who had loved me more than anyone. My whole life, until this point, had been a total nightmare that affected everyone who met me.

More time passed, and I finally got the courage to ask if I could see him. When I finally did, I fell at my grandfather's feet and could only cry loudly and uncontrollably. He cried with me. Eventually I got out between sobs how sorry I was for what I had done, and then I told him that Jesus had saved me.

He said, "Son, I have prayed for you all of your life. I could not take watching you destroy yourself any longer, and I finally gave you over to God. If this is what it took for you to give your life to Him, I wish it would have happened years ago!" He was absolutely forgiving, just as the Lord had been to me.

Grandpa lived four more years, and they were the best we ever had together. He saw me marry a wonderful Christian woman. He held our newborn son, whom we named after him. He lived to see my wife pregnant with our daughter before he died. Unbelievably, he even left me in charge of everything he owned, despite the life I had led.

I was so full of joy that I could live without substance abuse and hate. I asked God that I be able to help others find the same joy. He has granted my prayers again.

Today I am the president and cofounder of a residential recovery program. We have live-in recovery for those addicted to alcohol and drugs. We also have a counseling center that deals with drug- and alcohol-related issues, as well as many other issues people may have. I know that God has given me this calling. We are building our second four-story facility in Gainesville, and we have been blessed to see many lives changed. Nothing gives me greater joy today than to see a guy turn his life around and give it over to the Lord.

Jesus reminds me that "to whom much is given, much is required." And I have been given much.

My prayer today is that my life will give the Lord glory, and that my testimony will help those who struggle from a life without hope to find true hope and healing in the Lord Jesus Christ.

I close by saying that I don't care how far you have gone—I know Jesus is waiting with open arms to forgive you and receive you, just as He did me. I also know that He will, if you will only ask Him.

6. One Way

Tom McAllister

You may have heard the saying, "There's more than one way to skin a cat." In order to achieve PETA-approved political correctness, I guess I should have chosen another phrase, but that was the first adage to come to mind, and it fits. Actually, I think the reference to "cat" refers to a catfish, so since there's no fur involved, perhaps they won't mind.

Anyway, it means that there is more than one way to do something. In the military, we used to say that there was a right way, a wrong way, and the military way, which always seemed somewhere in between. Here's one unofficial navy slogan promoting this perception: *The Navy: over 200 years of tradition unmarred by progress.*

In professional consulting, the term "*best practices*" is repeated almost ad nauseam. That's the purpose of a consultant, however: they are subject-matter experts on their particular field of endeavor and have to be able to complete a task or set of tasks in not just any way, but in the best way possible—typically in terms of quality, cost, and speed.

In travel, there always seem to be multiple ways to get to a place. Any GPS unit can calculate multiple routes for you based on pre-programmed priorities such as shortest driving distance or maximizing the use of interstate highways.

In the spiritual realm, are there many paths to God? If all roads lead to Rome, then do all paths lead to God? Is there a "best practices" path—one that is simply better than the others? Perhaps it is a blended solution where each faith has some things right and some things wrong, so if you piece all the right stuff together in the right way, then you'll have the grand answer—the spiritual equivalent of a World Religion *Greatest Hits* CD. These are important points to ponder.

If we follow this culture's obsession with political correctness, then the answer must be "yes" to the multiple-paths-to-God question. It would be politically incorrect to say otherwise. It doesn't take much scholarly analysis, however, to recognize that this is impossible. Some religions say that there is only one God, while others proclaim many gods ranging from a few to over a million. *Somebody* has miscounted. Some faiths promote the idea of a unique soul belonging to each individual while others promote a recycled soul (reincarnation). Both of these beliefs may be wrong, but both cannot be right–if one is correct, the other must be wrong. Some faiths promote an afterlife while others do not. Of those that support some type of afterlife, all but Christianity believe that some method of measuring people's good works versus their bad determines their final destination in this next life. Christianity claims that all of us are unworthy of heaven, but that faith in Christ *makes* us worthy, and is the only road to salvation. The deeper you go, the more incompatible the various faiths become. Most are outright mutually exclusive of each other. In other words, believing in one faith makes believing in another faith impossible. There may, in fact, be many paths to God, but it seems that all but one must have a Bridge Out Ahead sign somewhere along the way. In the final analysis, the politically correct assertion that everyone is right in their religion is a lie.

So what is true? What is the one right path to God? We get to choose what we believe, but that choice shouldn't be based on our whims, family upbringing, or what best fits our desired lifestyle. It should be based on the truth, and it's incumbent upon all of us to seek that truth with all our heart. You have the Talmud, the Koran, Buddha's

Four Noble Truths, the Bible, and others to explore. Investigate them all if you are unsure, for it is incredibly important that you choose the right path. No one wants to go down a road to God only to discover that its bridge is out and you fall into Monty Python's "gorge of eternal peril."

All things equal, the "best practices" recommendation would be to start with Christianity, as it not only has the largest number of followers, but virtually all the other religions view the Christian Savior, Jesus Christ, as at least a holy man or prophet. This streamlines your investigation efforts in terms of quality, cost, and speed. The crux of the matter quickly becomes, "Is Jesus just a holy man or prophet no different than Moses, Buddha, Mohammed, or any other celebrated religious figure? Or is He the Son of God?"

The Bible is quite clear on who Jesus is and what the correct road to salvation is. There is no ambiguity or an allusion to an alternate back road. There is only one path. We have a Creator Who desires a relationship with us. He loves us so incredibly much that He wants us to address Him as Father. He wants us to know His Son, and He makes it very clear through His inspired Word that His Son is the Way to Him:

> "But as many as received Him, to them He gave the right to become children of God, even to those who believe in His name" (John 1:12 NASB).
>
> "Whoever believes in the Son has eternal life, but whoever rejects the Son will not see life, for God's wrath remains on him" (John 3:36 NIV).
>
> "You search the Scriptures because you think that in them you have eternal life; it is these that testify about Me; and you are unwilling to come to Me so that you may have life" (John 5:39–40 NASB).
>
> "I tell you the truth, he who believes has everlasting life" (John 6:47 NIV).
>
> "I am the door; if anyone enters through Me, he will be

saved, and will go in and out and find pasture" (John 10:9 NASB).

"Jesus said to her, 'I am the resurrection and the life; he who believes in Me will live even if he dies, and everyone who lives and believes in Me will never die. Do you believe this?'" (John 11:25–26 NASB).

"Jesus did many other miraculous signs in the presence of His disciples, which are not recorded in this book. But these are written that you may believe that Jesus is the Christ, the Son of God, and that by believing you may have life in His name" (John 20:30–31 NIV).

"And there is salvation in no one else; for there is no other name under Heaven that has been given among men by which we must be saved" (Acts 4:12 NASB).

"Of Him all the prophets bear witness that through His name everyone who believes in Him receives forgiveness of sins" (Acts 10:43 NASB).

"We believe that we are all saved the same way, by the undeserved grace of the Lord Jesus" (Acts 15:11 NLT).

"They replied, 'Believe in the Lord Jesus, and you will be saved—you and your household" (Acts 16:31 NIV).

"In Him we have redemption through His blood, the forgiveness of our trespasses, according to the riches of His grace" (Eph. 1:7 ESV).

"And the testimony is this, that God has given us eternal life, and this life is in His Son. He who has the Son has the life; he who does not have the Son of God does not have the life. These things I have written to you who believe in the name of the Son of God, so that you may know that you have eternal life" (1 John 5:11–13 NASB).

"For I am not ashamed of this Good News about Christ. It is the power of God at work, saving everyone who believes—the Jew first and also the Gentile" (Rom. 1:16 NLT).

"For the wages of sin is death, but the gift of God is eternal life in Christ Jesus our Lord" (Rom. 6:23 NIV).

"Whoever will call on the name of the Lord will be saved" (Rom. 10:13 NASB).

"Now, brothers, I want to remind you of the gospel I preached to you, which you received and on which you have taken your stand. By this gospel you are saved, if you hold firmly to the word I preached to you. Otherwise, you have believed in vain. For what I received I passed on to you as of first importance: that Christ died for our sins according to the Scriptures" (1 Cor. 15:1–3 NIV).

"Jesus gave His life for our sins, just as God our Father planned, in order to rescue us from this evil world in which we live" (Gal. 1:4 NLT).

"I am shocked that you are turning away so soon from God, who called you to Himself through the loving mercy of Christ. You are following a different way that pretends to be the Good News but is not the Good News at all. You are being fooled by those who deliberately twist the truth concerning Christ. But even if we or an angel from Heaven should preach a gospel other than the one we preached to you, let him be eternally condemned" (Gal. 1:6–8 NLT).

"You are all sons of God through faith in Christ Jesus" (Gal. 3:26 NIV).

"This is a trustworthy saying, and everyone should accept it: 'Christ Jesus came into the world to save sinners'— and I am the worst of them all" (1 Tim. 1:15 NLT).

"For there is one God and one mediator between God and men, the man Christ Jesus" (1 Tim. 2:5 NIV).

"And from Jesus Christ, the faithful witness, the firstborn

of the dead, and the ruler of the kings of the earth. To Him Who loves us and released us from our sins by His blood" (Rev. 1:5 NIV).

"Blessed be the God and Father of our Lord Jesus Christ, Who according to His great mercy has caused us to be born again to a living hope through the resurrection of Jesus Christ from the dead, to obtain an inheritance which is imperishable and undefiled and will not fade away, reserved in Heaven for you" (1 Peter 1:3–4 NASB).

The Bible is a love story about the Creator in continual pursuit of His created. Our Heavenly Father loves us and desires that no one should perish, but that all receive eternal life. He has provided through inspiration over 400 verses (according to Dr. Jack Van Impe's count, and he can probably recite them all) of Scripture that tell us exactly how. "How do I love thee? Let me count the ways." Here's the main one:

"For God so loved the world that He gave His only begotten Son, that whoever believes in Him shall not perish, but have eternal life" (John 3:16 NASB).

This is an incredible act of love that God the Father would sacrifice His Son in order to have a relationship with us. Now think logically about this for a moment and consider this hypothetical scenario. Let's say you were a parent of a male child with a special characteristic and suddenly the entire world was infected with a deadly virus. All of humankind would die in a matter of weeks, and the only cure was something absolutely unique in your child's blood that could produce a vaccine that would save the planet. In order to produce this vaccine, your child had to die. Now how's that for a parental dilemma? To save the human race, you must sacrifice your son.

Would you do it?

You certainly wouldn't even consider it if there was another way.

Do you think that God, all-knowing and all-loving, would have sacrificed His Son if there was an alternative method? Would Jesus have surrendered His life for our sakes if there was a backdoor route into salvation? He even prayed fervently, sweating blood, asking the Father if there was another way. There was no other way. If there was, then Jesus' sacrificial death on the cross would not have been required. Even within our limited intellectual capacity, we should easily grasp this logical truth.

Do you want to know the one way, the only way to God? "Jesus answered, 'I am the Way and the Truth and the Life. No one comes to the Father except through Me'" (John 14:6 NIV). There is no bridge out on His path. He is the road to the Father; He is the way to life eternal. All other paths will come to a dead end, but when you travel with Jesus, you will always get to the right destination.

7. Knock! Knock!

Tom McAllister

You never know when an opportunity will present itself. The saying "I'd rather be lucky than good" is amusing, but banking on random good fortune is a low-percentage bet. As a general principle, we should all follow the motto of the Boy and Girl Scouts: *Be Prepared.* Preparation enables us to recognize an opportunity and take advantage of it. Being lucky is more than simply being in the right place at the right time. Even if people are in a fortunate circumstance, if they don't recognize the opportunity or have failed to prepare themselves to take advantage of it, then that opportunity will slip away from them. In many cases, they won't even know that they missed it.

In the business world, experienced salespeople know this. There are often small windows of time when they have a chance to discuss their product or service to a potential customer. A good salesman will rehearse for this opportunity so that he is able to describe the features and benefits of his product or service in a short and concise manner. It's often called the "elevator pitch" as the duration is about the length of time of an elevator ride. It's rare that anyone can *close* a deal in such a short span, though closing is the ultimate goal. However, in this brief encounter, the initial objective is to plant enough seeds, pique enough curiosity, and provide enough interest that a follow up meeting can occur.

In our general walk in life, we are all salesmen. We communicate our ideas in persuasive speech; we present our opinions and thoughts to gain the acceptance of others, and we invite them to participate in our plans. Sometimes we "sell" passively by our actions and by how others interpret those actions.

Those of us who are Christians are all tasked to be salespeople. It's part of our job description as followers of Christ. Check it out:

> "Therefore, go and make disciples of all nations, baptizing them in the name of the Father and of the Son and of the Holy Spirit, and teaching them to obey everything I have commanded you. And surely I am with you always, to the very end of the age" (Matt. 28:19–20 NIV)
>
> But you will receive power when the Holy Spirit comes on you; and you will be My witnesses in Jerusalem, and in all Judea and Samaria, and to the ends of the earth (Acts 1:8 NIV).

Jesus' words in the verses above are referred to as the Great Commission. They were the last words that He spoke to His followers before He ascended into Heaven. It's not the Great Suggestion. When the Son of God says to do something, it's a command.

We need to be good Scouts and be prepared to witness to others. Create and rehearse your elevator pitch. Think of why you put your trust in Jesus, and be able to explain it in a simple way. This will accomplish two things: First, it confirms your own beliefs and arranges them into a logical and persuasive order, which should strengthen your own faith. Second, it enables you to give a confident answer to the questioner, which should further elevate his or her interest.

Even though Peter was a simple fisherman, he understood this. He wrote, "But in your hearts set apart Christ as Lord. Always be prepared to give an answer to everyone who asks you to give the reason for the hope that you have. But do this with gentleness and respect" (1 Pet. 3:15

NIV). The apostle Paul offers similar advice, "Let your conversation be always full of grace, seasoned with salt, so that you may know how to answer everyone" (Col. 4:6 NIV).

Many are uncomfortable discussing their faith. You might be concerned that you won't give the right answers, or you may be afraid of what people will ask, or how they will respond. Just speak the truth in love (gentleness and respect) from your heart, and let the Holy Spirit speak through you. He will guide you. Start with your "elevator pitch" and let it flow from there. If the conversation gets difficult, then suggest a follow-up meeting where you can bring another witness, or simply invite them to church where they can request a meeting with one of the church staff.

Also, remember that what you do is at least as important as what you say. You can be a successful salesperson without saying a word—just let your actions speak for you. As Jesus said in the Sermon on the Mount: "Let your light shine before men in such a way that they may see your good works, and glorify your Father Who is in Heaven" (Matt. 5:16 NASB). People observe what you do and how you act. Make sure you behave "in such a way" that brings glory to God—that you honor Him with righteous living, simply loving and treating others as well as you would treat yourself, and loving God with all you've got.

Actions speak louder than words, but be prepared for the opportunity to witness to those who may come and ask why you are the way you are. Have your elevator pitch at the ready to explain why you believe the way you believe. It may be just a planting of the seed, which someone else may water and another harvest—or it might be harvest time right then. Then you can be a chosen vessel of God to lead another soul to the Lord. Now, how cool is that? To close a deal for Christ.

8. The News

Emmett Holley

"*It's* cancer and you're going to do *what?*"

Let me start this story by telling you that I am no one of any significance in this world. I am just your ordinary guy with an everyday existence, which means that I work a lot and don't get to play a lot. I was raised in a Christian home with two parents, Bill and Nell who were better than I deserved. I got married and have a beautiful wife, Ellen, and two wonderful children Jessica and Will. With all that said, I consider myself to be greatly successful. On a scale of one to ten, my faith in God had only been stress-tested to around a two because everything had gone pretty well in my life. I guess I thought that I didn't need much faith.

On a warm Sunday afternoon in October 2006 around 4:45 p.m., I received a phone call that would rock my world. I had just had surgery on my left eye to remove a "routine cyst" or tumor. It had bothered me for a few months, and finally my wife had hounded me into finding out what was going on. The eye doctor had determined that the cyst/tumor was behind my left eye and needed to be removed. He had referred me to an eye surgeon who had agreed with the original diagnosis. The surgeon, Dr. Vorno had reassured me that these types of tumors

45

were almost never cancerous. I honestly didn't expect there to be any problems.

I woke up from a surgery that seemed to last only a few minutes to find Ellen and Dr. Vorno standing beside my bed. My wife said that Dr. Vorno had some concerns. He said that the tumor looked suspicious. Even after being heavily sedated for a couple of hours, I could sense that the word *suspicious* was not a good thing. Later, I found out that Dr. Vorno had only cut the area open and closed it right back up after taking some tissue samples. I would be home for the next couple of days to recuperate with a patch over my left eye. Of course, there were some crazy thoughts going through my mind as to what was going on, but I figured that I wouldn't hear anything at least until Monday. After all, my surgery was on a Friday morning and I assumed that the doctors would be home for the weekend.

When the phone rang on Sunday afternoon, I saw on the Caller ID that it was the hospital, and I immediately answered. Much to my surprise, the voice on the other end belonged to Dr. Vorno who had performed the surgery—and he didn't sound as if he had just won the lottery. In a slow, broken voice, he said that the tumor was cancerous, and due to the type of cancer it was, in all likelihood, they would need to remove everything around the eye socket—including my eye.

"It's cancer and you're going to do *what?*" I asked. As tears started down my face and the words began to sink in, my heart sank to the lowest point in my life. I shook with fear and a chill ran up my spine like I have never felt before. Despite the fact that all kinds of people had conquered cancer and lived to tell their stories, in my mind, cancer was a death sentence, the end of life as I knew it. I hung up the phone and ran into my Ellen's arms. She already knew from my expression what the news was.

Dear God, please help me understand what is going on here? Confusion, frustration, fear, and a hundred other feelings rushed through my body. *I am just forty-four years old,* I thought. *I want to see my son and daughter graduate from high school, get married, and have kids. I have so many things that I need to take care of---I don't even have a will. What about growing old with my wife and working on my never-ending honey-do list?*

Needless to say, I was seriously overwhelmed with a severe panic attack. I can only imagine what was going through the minds of my wife and children. As a Christian, I knew in my heart that if I died, I would be going to Heaven (or at least cleaning up around outside the gates or something). However, I had not planned for this to happen in the next couple of months. I had not even considered yet what it would be like to have just one eye.

Since becoming a Christian, I learned that letting go and letting God control my life was the best decision that I could ever make. I realized through several "God Rescues" in my life that I wasn't the one driving my life's taxi—God was. I had made Him stop in a few places along the way where He didn't want to stop, but He had always been there waiting for me to get back in the cab after I screwed everything up. He has always been willing to take me back to fix me back up and get me back on the road again. He has also sent some angels into my life as well. One angel, who is a dear sweet woman that goes to church with my mother, gave me a scripture that I have never forgotten: I like the version that comes from the new Bible, *The Message,* most. The scripture is Proverbs 3:5–6:

> "Trust God from the bottom of your heart; don't try to figure out everything on your own. Listen for God's voice in everything you do, everywhere you go; He's the One Who will keep you on track."

It's pretty neat that God allowed me to remember this particular verse of scripture given the circumstances. Most of the time it takes me five minutes to find my wallet and truck keys in the morning and then leave only to discover that my fresh cup of coffee that I had prepared was left sitting on the kitchen countertop.

I knew that given this situation I would definitely have to have some help figuring out what was going on. For this task, God sent me another angel. Her name is Lynne. She and her husband had been what you might call our spiritual best friends for a great part of our life. Lynne came over and listened, cried, and even laughed with me for a while, but more than anything she helped me to understand what I had to do next. She told me that I had to "give this situation to God." Of course in the past, I would give everything to God with ten fingers attached to it so that hopefully "God" would make everything turn out the way I wanted it to. This time was different. I knew that I wasn't even capable of keeping ten fingers attached to it, and my walnut-sized brain couldn't even begin to grasp what was going on. The following is the prayer I prayed:

Father, I don't know why, but I am praising You for this situation. I know that You love me, but I am very confused and need Your help with this. Please help me, Ellen, Jessica, and Will as we go through this together with You.

After I had finished praying, I sat quietly for a while waiting to see if God would reveal the wonderful answer that I needed. I have never heard God speak to me in an audible voice. If God *were* to speak to me in an audible voice, I would more than likely drop dead and meet Him face-to-face right then. However, God spoke to my heart, and said, "Emmett, I do love you, and I am going to take care of you. Believe it or not, I love your wife and children more than you do." I can't explain how God put this in my heart, but He did.

Very quickly, I was back for the surgery to have my eye removed and—we hoped--all of the cancer along with it. Over the next several months, I would go through thirty-two radiation treatments. My oncologist, Dr. Finch wanted to kill any possible cancer cells in that area of my head because of the proximity to my brain. My wife claims it fried the remaining two intelligent brain cells in my head.

During one of the countless visits back to the eye surgeon, Dr. Vorno had a slip of the tongue. He said, "We are going to leave the eye socket open for the next couple of years to observe it." At this point, I was a little confused by his comment and really thought the appointment was about how they would attempt a prosthetic eye. Then he said, "If you make it two years, we will figure out something then." The only word that I heard him say was *if*. That caused a sudden spike on the panic-meter. It was like the phone call that I had received at the beginning of my story. The phone was ringing again. *What now?* As I mentioned before, I had learned to let go and let God take control. He is driving, not me. God being the great Cabbie that He is, just turned around, smiled at me, and said, "Emmett, don't worry. Every day is a great day, whether I take you to your home or My home." That thought has comforted me to this day.

Well, it has been almost four years since my ordeal, and I must tell you how awesome God still is. I still have only one eye and really no hope for a prosthetic due to the extensive surgery, but God has allowed my heart to double in size. I now truly understand His saving grace, and feel His warm, loving embrace every day. He has shown me in countless ways how important each day is. I choose now to serve Him in a different way, and that is for Him to use me as His vessel. I am an imperfect vessel, but He still loves me and uses this worn, now-forty-eight-year-old vessel every day. I appreciate every moment of my cab ride, although I suspect that God might have kept me around so that He wouldn't have to do my honey-do list.

9. Give It Up

Tom McAllister

My great-grandfather, Harvey Caswell McAllister, served as a first lieutenant in the North Carolina 8th Regiment, Company H, in the War Between the States. History books refer to it as the American Civil War. Most Southerners refer to it as the War of Northern Aggression. He was a farmer, but he didn't own any slaves—he had nine kids instead. After the war, Harvey went into contracting and built the Lutheran church in Mount Pleasant, North Carolina, which still stands today. He served a couple of terms as a state legislator. There was nothing extravagant or flashy about my great-grandfather's life—just your good old-fashioned salt and light in the world.

As one of his descendants and part of the elect ("American by birth and Southern by the Grace of God"), I am absolutely galled to quote a Yankee general (a cigar-chomping, drunk one at that), whose soldiers were responsible for wounding ole Harvey twice (one in the knee, the other in the thigh) during the siege of Petersburg. Unfortunately, there are no more appropriate words to describe the attitude with which we should approach our Heavenly Father than the ones Gen. Ulysses. S. Grant used in the capture of Fort Donelson: *Unconditional Surrender.*

These words are even hard for me to type. They certainly don't roll easily off my tongue. There's something inside every human being—and not just those of Southern heritage—that makes it distasteful to us to give in. Perseverance is an excellent and godly trait. James, the Lord's brother, tells us to "let our perseverance grow, for when your endurance is fully developed, you will be perfect and complete, needing nothing" (James 1:4 NLT). The key is in the source of the motivation. Are we motivated to serve God or serve ourselves? It's been commented on for decades, but we are still deep into the evolution of the Me generation. It's all about us. We perceive everything from our myopic point of view—from the most important to the mundane. Our dedication is primarily egocentrically driven.

Have you ever been in a group photo? Who's the first person you look for? It's not "Look at Fred acting crazy" or "What's up with Suzy's hair?" Those comments may come later, but the first thing you look for in the photo is you. We're hardwired that way. It's part of our fallen state. Our greatest interest is ourselves.

In his bestseller, *The 7 Habits of Highly Effective People,* Stephen Covey teaches that we all act based on our "centers." We are all centered on something, (our work, our money, our relationships, ourselves, etc.). Covey argues that we will be happiest and most successful when we are *principle-centered* in our behavior.

Principles are a great start. Principles are like scientific laws. They are timeless in their application, universal in scope, and consistent in their results. They are not subject to the fickleness of emotions or the environment. If we choose biblical principles, it's even better. God built this universe, so He knows best how it operates. But the best alternative is to become *God-centered.*

Trying to manage our behavior by following a great set of principles means that we are still depending on our own abilities to complete a task properly. The objective is correct, but it remains centered on our own efforts to get there. We must put God at the top as our highest priority, and place Christ in the center of our hearts. We then surrender or submit our lives to Him. It's not about us; it's all about Him.

Dr. James Merritt once gave a sermon that provided a great analogy for this concept. Accepting Jesus Christ as your Lord and Savior is like having Jesus hand you a blank contract and telling you to sign it. Our first reaction is to think this is crazy. Nobody signs a blank contract. What's in it? What do I have to do? There's no small print; heck, there's no print at all! Who would do such a thing? But that's the deal. It is a total trust, a total commitment, and a total surrender to Him. It's investing all you got. Remember now, who you are signing this contract with. This is the One Who created the whole universe, and He loves you. He *died* for you!

When you surrender all to God, He will live through you, guide you, and direct you to places and accomplishments that you could never imagine. It is the best "contract" you'll ever sign.

When you accept Jesus Christ as your Savior, you become a new you—not a rebuilt you, but a whole new person and nature. ("Therefore, if anyone is in Christ, he is a new creation; the old has gone, the new has come" 2 Cor. 5:17 NIV.) You are made completely righteous in God's eyes. That's great news. So what do we do with that?

Well, we march out in our new nature trying to be good, and we fail. We try again, and we fail. We pray, we fast, and we fail some more. What is up with this? We think, *"How can I have a completely new nature and still be acting like the old me where I keep falling into sin and making mistakes?"* Our lives seem analogous to those horror movies, *Friday the 13th* or *Halloween* where you keep killing or getting rid of the boogie man and he keeps coming back to life to haunt you some more. We want to shout, *Just go away and die already!*

Even the mighty apostle Paul, author of half the New Testament, expressed in frustration this sentiment:

> I want to do what is good, but I don't. I don't want to do what is wrong, but I do it anyway. But if I do what I don't want to do, I am not really the one doing wrong; it is sin

living in me that does it. I have discovered this principle of life—that when I want to do what is right, I inevitably do what is wrong. I love God's law with all my heart. But there is another power within me that is at war with my mind. This power makes me a slave to the sin that is still within me. Oh, what a miserable person I am. Who will free me from this life that is dominated by sin and death? (Rom. 7:19–24 NLT).

His answer is in verse 25: "Thank God. The answer is in Jesus Christ our Lord" (NLT).

Our problem is that we focus on our *behavior* and not on our *belief.* This improper perception is probably the experience of the majority of the people brought up in the church. It's the Ten Commandments mindset with all the "Thy shalls" and "Thy shall nots." Obey this and don't do that. If our approach to life is trying to follow a set of rules using our own willpower in order to be obedient to God, then our life *will* be a miserable journey. However, when we focus our belief on the promises of God, our mindset totally changes. This isn't some idea based on the power of positive thinking. Saying "love one another" as opposed to "don't steal, lie, or cheat your neighbor" does have psychological benefits, but this is far deeper than positive thinking. Belief comes from our core being. If we believe that God loves us completely and cares for us intimately, and we believe that His Son's death on the cross guarantees us an eternal life, and if we believe that this new life is more joyful than the greatest feeling we've ever experienced here on earth, then this belief will totally change our perspective on life. We are loved, we are valued, and we are cherished by *Almighty God!* Truly believing this will drive our behavior.

Our behavior is always driven by our belief. In Bible lingo, belief begets behavior, and the greater the commitment to our belief, the greater the influence on our behavior. So we need to focus our hearts on Christ and not our heads on the Law or our attention on our action. This mindset or perspective is a heart and belief thing, not a muscle and do thing. Christ has already done all the work on the cross. Therefore, there is now no condemnation for those who are in Christ Jesus (Rom. 8:1 NIV). None. We are God's children, and we are promised full inheritance into His Kingdom.

It is this belief; this understanding that we are the children of God that will break the power of sin in our lives. We are no longer our old nature—the one that was a slave to sin. We are reborn as a kid of the King! We are princes and princesses of the Heavenly Kingdom. We are incredibly loved, and we flourish in His court. Believing that we are God's children will change our behavior. Realizing that we are unconditionally loved will free us to fully love others. If we fill our hearts with the love of Christ, then our behavior will reflect that love. Wherever your heart is, that's where your treasure lies. Focus on your new awareness as a child of God, and you will begin to live out Jesus's new commandment: "Love one another as I have loved you" (John 13:34).

When we love God, we will want to please Him. Paul summarizes this approach in the first two verses of Romans 12 (NLT):

> Therefore, I urge you, brothers, in view of God's mercy, to offer your bodies as living sacrifices, holy and pleasing to God—this is your spiritual act of worship. Don't copy the behavior and customs of this world, but let God transform you into a new person by changing the way you think. Then you will learn to know God's will for you, which is good and pleasing and perfect.

When we surrender our will to God, He can use all of us for His glory. Our behavior is directed by our love for Him, and we will be motivated by a desire to do well as opposed to a fear of doing wrong.

Let's face it; God is a loving Father Who wants to bless us beyond our wildest dreams. His plan for us is far greater than anything we can conceive. (He's a bit wiser than we are.) Rest in the knowledge that Father knows best. Focus on Him, follow Him, and then leave all the consequences to Him. There is such freedom in this! Simply follow Christ, and He will assume responsibility for all outcomes. There is such peace in this! Even if we are enduring a difficult situation, God knows about it and He's in charge. We just need to take comfort; He's right here with us.

We may not always understand. His ways are not our ways, and sometimes it seems God has an ironic sense of humor. In order to be the greatest, you must act like the least; in order to receive, you give; and in order to achieve ultimate freedom and victory, you surrender unconditionally.

So smile as you pick up your cross daily and follow Him. You're on the road to victory! Give it up for the Lord, and you will receive His abundant blessings in this journey of life and in His Kingdom to come.

10. Name Calling

Tom McAllister

"What's in a name? That which we call a rose by
any other name would smell as sweet."
—William Shakespeare, *Romeo and Juliet*

So how important is a name? Is the Bard of Avon also the Bard and Brains of Branding? For new companies, branding is considered a very important enterprise as the brand is the initial image the consumer sees—the opening statement about your company. If a rose was actually called a pukglobenstinke, it may smell as sweet, but perhaps few would dare try to take a whiff of it.

According to *Business Week* in 2009, the value of just the name, Coca-Cola, is worth over $68 billion. That's a lot of soda. Other top company brand names are IBM, Microsoft, Nokia, McDonald's, and Google. Proverbs states, "A good name is more desirable than great wealth. Respect is better than silver or gold" (Prov. 22:1 GWT). From this analysis, it seems a good name is great wealth.

So is the value of their company caused by their name? Or has the value and quality of what they do and the goods and services they provide caused their name to have value?

Although a catchy jingle, name, logo, or slogan can enhance a company's overall marketing, the major metric for the value of a name is based on the quality of how the company performs. If its smell is desirably sweet, even a pukglobenstinke will develop a loyal sniffing fan base. It is who the company is, what it represents, what it does, and how well it does it that makes a good name.

When Enron became an infamous name, Arthur Andersen, a multi-billion dollar "Big Five" consulting firm was handling much of Enron's accounting practices and books. The Arthur Andersen firm started in the early 1900s and developed a reputation for honesty and a zeal for maintaining high standards within the accounting industry. For many years, their motto was, "Think straight, talk straight."[1]

However, when faced with the conflict of following proper accounting practices and reporting procedures or trying to enhance their client's financial position, the Andersen firm chose unwisely. After the Enron scandal broke, the company went from think straight, talk straight to straight down the tubes. The end came quickly as most of the business was sold off to other accounting firms. Although the firm has never formerly closed or gone into bankruptcy, in a period of about eighteen months it went from over 100,000 employees worldwide to now around 200.[2]

Arthur Andersen lost its good name.

On the *O'Reilly Factor* on the Fox News Channel, host Bill O'Reilly bragged about the Fox cable channel being the most trusted name in news as 49 percent of Americans trusted Fox. This was way ahead of CNN and more than twice that of MSNBC. Fox is proud of being the leader as they claim to be the most "fair and balanced," but in general, it is still an honor among thieves. The sad fact is that over 50 percent of Americans don't trust Fox, and they trust the other networks even less. The mainstream media industry should be ashamed of their loss of integrity and trust from the American people. To quote Bernie Goldberg, the mainstream media has become the "lame-stream media," and the entire industry has lost its good name.

The current public opinion of our members in Congress is at an all-time low, and this rating has been down for several years. The American citizenry watch with disdain the appalling behavior of our politicians. We see their backroom deals, schmoozing with special interest groups. We see their motivation for self-preservation and priority for their party over the people of this country. They are public servants elected to provide a public service. Yet, they possess and project this arrogant attitude of "public, serve us." Our elected leaders are losing their good name.

On the individual level, this can happen to us, too. Our name is all that we have in this world, and we should be very careful to protect it. Although there are lots of Peters, Pauls, and Johns in the world, not many parents name their kids Judas these days. Sometimes a stain lasts forever.

We should be wise in how we walk in this life and careful in what we do. We should protect our name and ensure that it is esteemed with honor, integrity, and righteousness. Jesus told His disciples, "Whoever wants to be the most important person must take the last place and be a servant to everyone else" (Mark 9:35 GWT). Never let greed surpass integrity. Never compromise or shortcut your values and principles to achieve an objective. Be kind and treat others with respect and honor. Perform the Golden Rule of do unto others what you would want them to do unto you. Another proverb states, "Never let loyalty and kindness leave you. Tie them around your neck as a reminder. Write them deep within your heart. Then you will win favor and a good name in the sight of God and man" (Prov. 3:3–4 NLT).

These are not hard concepts to understand, but if you are not careful, they can be hard concepts to continuously follow. Sometimes it only takes one slip, and a great reputation can be forever tarnished. As the saying goes, it takes only one "Aw shucks" to wipe out ten "attaboys."

So don't shuck things up—protect your "brand name" and honor God with it.

11. Driving Range

Tom McAllister

John Weber, the pastor of Christ our Shepherd Lutheran church where I had just started attending, was teaching a class to new members. He was addressing the root cause of our troubles here on this earth. The class he was teaching was on the topic of sin. He wrote the word on the board as follows:

s I n

The basic problem of sin is our overemphasis on the "I." When it comes to sin, the "I's" have it. It's a focus on ourselves from our perspective and our priorities. In our fallen state, we start out that way. It's embedded within our corrupt nature. We can blame it on Adam, but it doesn't change our status: we begin life in this world self-centered, and some of us never grow out of it.

God knows our condition. He is perfectly holy, and we are not. We are spiritually separated from God, and we cannot have a relationship with Him in our present condition, because having a relationship requires a connection, a bond. Someone who is perfectly holy cannot connect with someone who is unholy without affecting His perfect Holiness. When confronted with perfect holiness, the unholy gets obliterated. As imperfect beings, we'd be like a bug hitting a bug zapper—and we'd be zapped. But God loves us, and He desires a relationship with us.

He loves us so much that He gave His only Son to die for us, so that whoever believes in Him shall not perish, but have eternal life (John 3:16). Through Christ, we can have a relationship with Holy God.

From the moment we accept Jesus Christ as our Lord and Savior, our entire relationship with God changes. "Therefore, there is now no condemnation for those who are in Christ Jesus" (Rom. 8:1 NIV), and through Christ's death on the cross, we are presented "holy in God's sight, without blemish and free from accusation" (Col. 1:22). All our sins are blotted out, and He forgets them completely. God now sees us as holy, thanks to Jesus, and therefore we can come into His presence and have a direct relationship with the Father.

So what about sin? Well, we can still screw up. From the believer's perspective, sin is like a bad golf shot. In most cases, we recognize it right away. Sometimes, we even suspect that we're lined up wrong, but we swing at the ball anyway. The results are predictable. Depending upon your level of self-control (a fruit of the Spirit), you may slam your club and/or immediately vocalize, often in colorful language, your opinion of the outcome, but in a short time, you regain your composure. You rethink the mechanics and your swing thoughts, evaluate what went wrong, and then make the appropriate adjustments. The next step, as most golfers will tell you, is crucial: *Learn from it, forget about it,* and *focus on your next shot.* Dwelling on your mistake will cloud your mind and attitude, and it will adversely affect your game. Dwelling on a sin after you've repented and made amends for the damage you caused serves no purpose either. *Fix your divot and move on.* God remembers your sins no more, so why should you?

For both believers and nonbelievers, there are consequences to our bad shots (sins) in life. From the worldly prospective, your errant shot may end up out of bounds or with a difficult lie that you must deal with. But here's the good news for those who have accepted Christ as Savior: God doesn't count the stroke against you. Your sins (or excess strokes) are forgiven. Through the amazing grace of our Lord, you get unlimited mulligans. When Christ died for us on the cross, all our sins were forgiven. Every sin we have committed, are committing, and ever will commit are washed clean from His shed blood. How's that for a loving and gracious Father? That while we are yet sinners, Christ died for us (Rom. 5:8), and He has cleansed us from all unrighteousness (1 John 1:9).

If you're not a golfer, then use a car expense account analogy. In our journey through life, anytime we sin, there's a vehicle expense. With Christ, we have an unlimited budget, and He picks up the tab.

"Well, holy blank check!" we might say. "Whether on the golf course or on the road, let's just drive however we want."

Hold on there, tiger. Think about this a moment. Is this the smart way to play? Like the majority of the automobile commercials advise us, "Your mileage may vary depending upon how your drive." This approach is not only less productive; it's disingenuousness. Driving however you want is the "secret agent in disguise" methodology. That's where you say that you are a believer in Christ, yet your actions speak otherwise. You go around and introduce yourself: "The name's Bondage. James Bondage—license to sin."

This is not the best course of action. Virtually all of us golfers do not tee up our ball and intentionally drive it into the woods. We do that often enough without trying. If you had a really expensive car, such as a Ferrari, Bentley, Lamborghini, AC Cobra, or Corvette, would you trash it just because you could afford to have it repaired? Most would say no. Well then, to go on living in sin when you have accepted Christ as your Lord doesn't make any sense either.

During my last tour of duty in the U.S. Navy, an Air Force major friend of mine and I traveled together to teach a class on military logistics at the U.S. Marine base in Albany, Georgia. One evening, as we headed out to dinner, she asked me an interesting question that some of you may have heard before. "If you were on trial for being a Christian, would there be enough evidence to convict you?"

After a moment of contemplation, I replied, "Yes, if the court could see my heart." She replied that this was a great answer, yet I felt inwardly embarrassed by it, which was her intention. It was her subtle way of speaking the truth in love to a fellow "golfer" who she saw was still "shanking shots" out on the golf course of life. I also immediately recognized my inconsistency. At the time, I still had a large amount of carnality in my Christian walk. Her question served as a mirror for me to see myself. Why would I believe in Christ, yet be so easily seduced by the call of the wild? The Holy Spirit often provides conviction in unusual circumstances. My spirit was willing, but my flesh was weak, and I had no real intent for an exercise plan to make it any stronger. I had no doubt that Jesus Christ was the Son of God who died for me, but I was pretty much driving however I wanted. I was James Bondage, and subsequently, I spent a fair amount of time in the rough.

There are many reasons why we can be in secret-agent-for-Christ mode. Perhaps the most common is all the distractions of the world. Busyness is the enemy of intimacy. It's tough to have a close relationship with the Father and a strong prayer life when you have a hard time getting Him on the calendar. In addition to this, without being deeply rooted in Christ, the lure of the world can overwhelm our old, sinful nature. Even the wisest man of all, Solomon, eventually succumbed to this temptation by having his heart led astray. Of course, he had seven hundred wives and another three hundred mistresses (concubines) to deal with. If trying to love two women is like a ball and chain, as the Oak Ridge Boys sang, then trying to love a thousand must be like having the planet Jupiter strapped to your leg.

Another reason we sometimes go into secret-agent mode is because we are not studying His Word in the Bible. Right after I finished college in 1983, I was sworn in as a navy officer. I attended the Navy Supply Corps School in Athens, Georgia. This is the home of the University of Georgia Bulldogs, where the greeting, "How 'bout them dawgs?" is spoken more prevalently than "Hello." Being a graduate of their instate rival, Georgia Tech, I thought that having to spend six months deep in "enemy territory" would certainly qualified me for hazardous duty pay. Unfortunately, the Navy didn't agree. Anyway, one day we had finished a class a few minutes early, so the class of about thirty student officers started talking about an important topic: football. One student brought up that on several occasions he had seen someone holding up a sign lettered John 3:16. He wanted to know what that was.

We students looked inquisitively at each other. Only one out of the thirty people in the class knew what the verse said. Only *one* out of thirty and I wasn't that person. It wasn't because of my upbringing. Our family went to church regularly. It was a Lutheran church, and if you're familiar with that type of service, it is very structured. Lutherans are like the teenage version of Catholics. The service has a lot of repetitive sayings, confession of sins, standing up, sitting down, kneeling, standing back up—if you threw in some ab crunches, you'd have a Pilates class. There are tons of scripture quoted repeatedly week after week and none of it stuck. I could repeat the sayings, but I didn't even know that it was verses of scripture because I was not studying His Word.

Paul's second letter to Timothy states "All Scripture is inspired by God and is profitable for teaching, for reproof, for correction, for training in righteousness" (2 Tim. 3:16 NASB). God's book is to be read on a routine basis and not serve as a static display on a tabletop or shelf. It's the playbook for living life well, and ignorance of it will cause one's faith to be a mile wide and an inch deep. Such a shallow knowledge of God's instructions and principles makes one highly vulnerable to deception.

Finally, the most difficult aspect of being a secret Christian is the lack of commitment. God is not looking for part-time employees. He wants His followers to be "all in," 24 hours a day, 7 days a week. Christianity is not a religion, but a way of life centered on a relationship with the Creator of the universe. It's a methodology of the heart. When we remove the "I" from the center of our lives and replace it with Christ, then we have the proper alignment and perspective that God desires. Some grasp this rather quickly, while many of us struggle through years of oscillating allegiance between God and our own desires to figure this out.

The theory and logic are not too hard to grasp. God knows all and can do all. He loves you far more than anyone else does. He knows what is best for you and wants what is best for you. Therefore, you can choose to follow His advice and direction or go out and "swing away" on your own. If you choose your own path, He is patient with you. Sooner or later, you'll get tired of constantly playing from a bad lie.

It took many poor golf shots for me to figure this out. Hopefully, you'll catch on sooner. The grass is greener and nicer in the fairway, and when you dedicate your life to following Him, you'll spend a lot more time there.

If we have Christ at the center of our lives, will we hit 'em straight, make many birdies, and even soar (score) like eagles? When you have Christ at the center of your life, it's like having the wisest caddy living within you, leading you through every shot. So yes, you will score very well. There will still be times when you hit a shot down the middle that takes a bad bounce or ends up in a divot. God challenges and tests those whom He loves so that they will be better and more fruitful in their game. In the end, however, you will be pleased with your score. Looking back at the end of your life, you will realize that having Christ at your center was not just the fair way, but the only way to play.

12. Gone in 30 Seconds

Jack Wehmiller

I somehow knew that the six o'clock news was not telling us the whole story. From everything I had heard through emails and correspondence with fellow missionaries and a Pastor friend of mine, the Haitian earthquake of January 12, 2010, was affecting a lot more than the capital city of Port-au-Prince. On the island of Hispaniola, where survival for many was a moment-to-moment struggle on the best of days, there had to be a lot more going on than we were hearing about.

What was I supposed to do with these feelings? How was I supposed to help? One thing became clear: I felt compelled to leave my very comfortable place in Gainesville, Georgia. I had to go down there and see for myself. Retirement had given me the time and the resources to get involved and the call to help was too great for me to resist.

In the sixth chapter of the book of Isaiah, the Lord says to Isaiah, "Whom shall I send and who will go for us?" Isaiah responds, "Here I am, send me." That scripture became very real to me after the earthquake struck. Others were going to help provide relief, and yet while medical teams were leaving for Haiti every day, I was not hearing any reports of people going to Hispaniola's other nation, the Dominican Republic (D.R.), just over the mountains from Haiti. Pastor Pedro Johnson, a wonderful man living in the D.R. in the city of Barahona, told me that their hospitals were overflowing with Haitians. Knowing Pastor Pedro as well as I did and knowing that he was not prone to exaggeration, the situation sounded dire.

"Here I am, send me," became "Here I go" with supplies, prayers, and hope that I can make a difference. Little did I know of the heroes that I would meet on this trip. Little did I know of the life-changing experience I was about to have.

I landed in the Dominican capital of Santo Domingo and was picked up by a missionary from Puerto Rico. We went directly to one of the public hospitals in the city known as *The Cantreras*. I saw room after room and hallway after hallway filled with badly hurt Haitian men, women, and children. One area had eleven women on gurneys waiting for surgery. Remarkably, all of these people had somehow survived the ten hour-plus journey across the horrid pot-hole-laced roads from Haiti to Santo Domingo—but still they had to wait. The hospital staff told me through an interpreter that they would get to all of them, "in the next couple of days." I thought to myself, *Some of them won't make it two more days. Some will die in a foreign hospital hundreds of miles from their homes, and away from any of their surviving family and friends.*

My suspicions were confirmed about what was going on outside the immediate area of the quake. Next I pressed on to Barahona, just across the border from Haiti. Two more hospitals had the same problems.

At the Sanchez Hospital, Pastor Pedro and I were confronted with an entire wing of the hospital dedicated to Haitian people hurt on that fateful day. We were in a hospital, so I could only imagine what it was like in the villages. Not only was the hospital overwhelmed with the tremendous number of quake victims with amputated limbs and broken bones, but it was painfully obvious that there was little if any fresh water available for these folks. I knew there was a scripture that spoke of giving a cup of cool water in the name of Christ, and this was what needed to be done. For two days we did just that. Young and old alike got water, juice, and words of encouragement. They got comfort from the group of nurses who were there with me. These women were from all over South Georgia, and they too had come to do what they could to help. These were humble, loving women giving of both their time and resources when both were greatly needed. The more I watched these heroes remove stitches, replace bandages, and give general care, the more I understood Jesus' admonition, "When you do it unto the least of these, you are doing unto Me."

I came to know several of the people to whom we ministered. I learned their names, ages, and what they were doing when the earthquake hit. I found out about friends and family who had perished or were missing and in doing so was moved to an entirely new level of understanding God's grace. In the midst of all that had happened, many of these men and women had not lost sight of who they were in Christ. The immediate lesson for me was never to try to reduce God to something that I could understand. I was to simply accept the grace in my life just as these souls had done. Displaced as they were, injured as they were, and in many cases having nothing more than the clothes on their backs, I saw a most wonderful sight: their Bibles at their bedsides. Someone had taken a mission trip to their town and shared the Gospel. Someone had lived out the Great Commission. Someone had come to this part of the world with "living water." I was passing out small material blessings to a physically battered group of God's children. In return, I was receiving incredible spiritual blessings.

On one very special day, I had decided to bring an interpreter with me to make sure that I was able to communicate with those that I would meet. Little did I know what that decision would mean in my life. I met a young woman named Miguelina Site. She had gone to the market January 12, just as she always did. Thirty seconds later, her injuries were so severe that her left arm above the elbow and her right leg above the knee had to be amputated. I gave her water and a smile. She gave me much more in return. Through Patrick, my interpreter, who was moving from room to room with me, I was told that Miguelina sang beautifully.

I asked if she felt well enough to sing. She smiled, nodded yes, lifted her right hand in the air, and began to sing.

I have obviously not been to Heaven yet, but I now know what the music will be like. The entire song was in Creole, except the last three words. In broken English, Miguelina sang out, "Hallelujah, Hallelujah, Hallelujah." She looked at me again before closing her eyes to rest. I sat on the edge of her hospital bed, touched her lightly on the shoulder, and took in the enormity of that moment in my life. She understood the saving grace of Christ. It had become such a part of her that it was now sustaining her at an incredibly difficult time.

I went to minister and instead, my Haitian brothers and sisters ministered to me. I went to encourage and instead was encouraged. I took a simple cool drink of water and in return received a torrent of blessings. God was at work that morning in the Sanchez Hospital, Barahona, D.R. I learned a wonderful lesson from one of God's angels here on earth, and I will never be the same again. I understand much better than ever before the difference between a mountain and a molehill. My personal mountains appear much lower now and many of my molehills have ceased to exist. I went in hopes of being a small blessing to others. I came home incredibly blessed. I will go back to this part of the world many times---of that I am sure.

13. Truth or Consequences, Part I

Tom McAllister

It is interesting to note that many people have the misplaced concept that science and spiritual faith are at odds with each other. They consider that science is full of laws, experimental proofs, and mathematical equations that substantiate fact, whereas faith is a magical leap into the unknown with a hope and a prayer. Nothing could be further from the truth. In fact, that is exactly what they both seek—the truth. Science and faith—or religion, should we say, which represents the organized body of faith—are completely complementary, and both are in search of the same objective: They both seek the truth, the whole truth, and nothing but the truth, because falsehoods in either is both dangerous and detrimental. No religious person wants to believe in something false any more than a scientist wants to promote an inaccurate theorem. The truth is the ultimate prize for both, but the approach is often different. Science tends to ask the question of how, whereas religion tends to ask the question of why.

A commonly used example is if I wanted to make a pot of tea and I put a kettle of water on the stove to boil. Later, another person enters the room and asks why is there water boiling on the stove. One answer is that the conductive heat transfer from the gas flame has increased the enthalpy of the water to surpass the phase change energy requirement to cause the water to convert to steam; and the other is that I wanted to make a pot of tea.

The debate of science versus religion is like that. There does exist however, an ultimate truth. This is truth with a capital "T." It truly (pun intended) is the whole truth and nothing but the truth. It is Truth. No human knows this Truth; in fact, no one even comes close. There are far more unknowns than knowns. There are probably far more unknown unknowns (things we don't even know that we don't know) than what we know. Ignorance is bliss, you know (as evident with my beloved Georgia Bulldog friends, "Yeah buddy, how 'bout them dawgs?"). To know Truth requires omniscience. One must know everything about everything to know Truth. Now, just because we cannot know this Truth or even come close to the total knowledge required of omniscience doesn't mean we should throw up our hands in surrender and seek bliss via ignorance, although it does seem that a few people have pursued this strategy. ("What was that question again? Oh, yeah, 'How 'bout them dawgs?'").

As such, despite the absence of complete truth, many assertions can be made that help us understand why things are and how things work. In science, there is a path progression toward truth based on the level of knowledge obtained through the depth and breadth of experimental validation. Ideas start with a hypothesis, grow into a theory, and then become confirmed into law. We have laws of gravity, thermodynamics, electromagnetism, and others where repeated experimental validation and mathematical proofs confirm their status. Theories have less degree of certainty than laws, such as the theory of relativity, chaos theory, and evolutionary theory. These are classified as theories because substantial amounts of data obtained through experiment and mathematical models support the presumed conclusion, but some conjecture remains. A hypothesis is the infant form of a future theory where insufficient testing and analysis have yet to occur.

In religion, the approach to understanding why things are the way they are is analogous to the scientific approach, but obviously, they are not the same. They both use a sense of logic, but religion relies more on experience than experiment. To the hardcore scientist, that sounds a little flaky, as karma does not fit well into a test tube. Yet, experience is just as valid as experiment, even though it does not occur in a laboratory. Without experience and interpretation, the world becomes a very boring place. From the scientific perspective, hearing Jimmy Page of Led Zeppelin stroking his guitar riffs on "Stairway to Heaven," Lynyrd Skynyrd jamming on "Freebird," or listening to Beethoven's Fifth Symphony simply become vibrations in air of multiple frequency and amplitude. A Rembrandt or Picasso painting is merely chemicals of varying pigments spattered upon a canvas. That's pretty dull. Science cannot even "explain" a mere thought. They can adeptly illustrate the chemical reactions and electrical impulses taking place in the brain, but how that becomes an idea is beyond the reach of science. There is no experiment that can recreate or validate the dream you had last night. Science is suitable to depict your brain, but wholly inadequate to describe your mind. Combining experiment and experience together, however, adds richness and depth to understanding the truth and the existence of the real. The more tools we employ to view the world, the greater our understanding and perception of Truth is.

This combined approach is not uncommon in the everyday functions of our society. Think of a criminal trial. You have the CSI guys performing the science aspect in their analysis of the scene, ballistics testing, and gathering samples of DNA, and you have the testimony of eye witnesses (experience) and the evaluation of motive (interpretation) of the suspect. It takes all of these characteristics to get a more accurate picture of the truth.

Belief, however, in and of itself may be perfectly aligned, partially aligned, or in complete opposition to the truth. It depends on what you believe. In the general trade of stocks, the person selling believes the stock will go down while the one buying believes it will go up. One of them has to be wrong. A common fallacy is the sense that the intensity and sincerity of one's belief enhances its truth. Unfortunately, there is no correlation between the two. Another falsehood is that because belief is personal, it's a blank check for whatever one wants to believe, and it is impossible or politically incorrect to state that one belief is superior to another.

Most everyone has heard of the tooth fairy. If I were to believe in the tooth fairy with all my heart, it still wouldn't make the tooth fairy real. I could envision a grander role for my tooth fairy in that upon my death, she would escort me to the pearly (white) gates of Heaven where I would get my crown of gold. I could dream up wonderful things and believe in them with complete sincerity, but no amount of faith would make it true. Religious faith, like science, is only valid when it represents the truth. Truth is the universal measuring stick for everything.

Whether a scientist, a theologian, a blue-collar faith-walker, or anyone else, we should all seek the truth and let it establish our principles and guide our actions. Ignoring or denying the truth is never beneficial. We even have a name for that way of life as "living in denial." It's denial of what? It's the denial of truth, and those who live in denial will always struggle.

We each start out in this world with the common individual truth, "By the grace of God, I am what I am" (1 Cor. 15:10a). We are each unique, but all are born into sin, and none of us live our lives perfectly. The unfortunate truth is that the pay out or wages of our sin is death. Thanks to God's immeasurable grace, the story doesn't end there:

"But the gift of God is eternal life through Christ Jesus" (Rom. 6:23b).

"Truly, I tell all of you with certainty, the one who believes in Me has eternal life" (John 6:47 ISV).

Now that's something that should cause us to pause and listen. When Jesus, the Son of God, tells you to believe something with certainty, then accept that as an undeniable truth.

14. Priority Check

Rick Saltzer

I had a plan for Saturday:
    to complete a large to-do list –
a day for work and not for play,
    I plunged in while pumping my fist

Sweat was dripping all over me
    when I noticed my little boy
smiling at me excitedly,
    as if he had found a new toy

I'm sure I looked sort of confused
    as we knelt there out on the lawn –
I asked why he seemed so enthused –
    it was then I finally caught on

I'd promised since last September
    that "tomorrow" we would play ball –
I didn't think he would remember,
    but this time he chose to recall

It was clear that I'd forgotten
    and had borne out my son's worst fears –
I stood there feeling plain rotten,
    watching his eyes filling with tears

As I worked, his eyes grew wetter,
    and even more so when I asked,
"Wouldn't tomorrow be better?" –
    and then I was fully unmasked

He stopped sobbing out of sheer pride,
    and fought to restrain his sorrow –
then he wiped his nose and replied,
    "Daddy, today *is* tomorrow" –

15. Child's Play

Tom McAllister

My dad was born in 1924, five years before the stock market crash and the start of the Great Depression. At the time of his birth, his father was fifty-two, and his mother was forty-two. Like many in rural North Carolina at that time, you didn't worry about getting to the hospital in time as he was conveniently born right there in the home. He was the last of nine kids, and naturally, being the baby of the family, he was the smartest and best looking...or so he told us. Being the youngest in his family, I had to agree (add smiley face here).

Dad had many of the stereotypical "growing up on the farm" stories—like walking two miles to school, barefoot, in the snow, uphill, both ways—but many of them were actually true. He did feed the chickens and milk the cows before school. The icebox was truly a box under the house with a big block of ice in it. His mom cooked over an open flame stove—not gas but wood-burning—and the house wasn't heated by a heat pump, but by multiple fireplaces, and all the wood needed to cook and heat the home wasn't cut by a chainsaw, but with an axe and a two-man crosscut saw.

Dad marveled that he probably had witnessed the greatest change in technology in human history as he went from plowing fields behind a horse, (or in some cases a mule) to watching a man land on the moon.

Having served in the U.S. Navy, my favorite story that Dad told me about his childhood was his excursion as an underwater diver. My dad's best friend growing up was his cousin Tom, for whom I am named. Tom later became a P-47 Thunderbolt pilot in World War II assigned to the 365th Fighter Group, the Hell Hawks. He was killed in action during the Invasion of Normandy on June 15, 1944. He was nominated for the DFC (Distinguished Flying Cross) for his actions in combat that day. The sad part of posthumous awards is the tremendous cost to receive them.

While they were growing up together, Tom and Dad were well known locally and were more commonly referred to as Frank and Jesse, as in Frank and Jesse James. They were a mischievous duo and pulled their fair share of pranks.

One time, while in an adventurous and inventive mood, Tom and my dad decided to try out underwater diving at the local pond down on the farm. The tools needed were an air source (bicycle pump), a long air hose, and a diving helmet. For the diving helmet, Dad "liberated" a large pot from his mom's kitchen. (When you come from a family of nine, there are lots of large pots around.) They cut a hole in the bottom of the pot and inserted a bicycle tire valve in the hole. This valve was connected to the long hose, which was connected to the bicycle pump. The concept was that one would wear the big pot over his head, go into the water, and just walk around on the bottom of the pond while the other would pump in air from the bicycle pump. Considering that the pot was metal, I don't know what they planned on "seeing" while walking on the bottom of the pond. (After listening to this story, I was really glad that Dad went into pharmacology and not engineering.) Now Tom was two years older than Dad, so when it came to who was selected for the "dangerous missions," Dad somehow was always chosen to be the test pilot, test diver, or whatever fancy title they used for the role, which in reality translated to "white rat."

When the day of the "big dive" arrived, Tom and Dad gathered on the little pier that jutted out a few yards from the edge of the pond. In order to make sure that Dad would sink to the bottom once he jumped into the water, they tied bricks to the bottom of his shoes. So now "Frank and Jesse" were ready for their first venture into underwater diving. Not even Norman Rockwell could picture this. Two young boys in overalls, standing out on a rickety little wooden pier, one manning a bicycle pump and the other with bricks tied to his shoes and a big metal pot on his head. (Alas, my dad was now a pothead.) Dad slowly shuffled out with his brick-laden shoes to the end of the pier. Tom was manning the bicycle pump, ready to start pumping as soon as Dad jumped in the water. I imagine there was a long, pregnant pause and several deep breaths once Dad reached the end of the pier. Yet with complete faith in his cohort, Dad jumped in.

I suppose that seeing a kid jump into a lake wearing a pair of old coveralls with bricks strapped to the bottom of his shoes and a big pot on his head might be quite amusing. It seems that was the case, because Tom didn't pump any air at all, but rolled on the pier laughing. The bricks did their job well, and Dad plunged rapidly to the bottom. The bottom of the pond was very soft mud, and the bricks sank in deep.

So now Dad was at the bottom of the pond, his feet tied to bricks that were stuck in the mud; he had a big pot on his head, and no air. When his feet wouldn't move, Dad got a little scared. He had to reach down, untie his shoelaces, and slip out of his shoes to swim up to the surface and breathe.

To add insult to this near-drowning experience, that night I think Dad got two whippings—one for cutting a hole in his mom's pot and the other for losing his shoes. Hearing stories like this made our family amazed that he made it to old age.

The other truly amazing part of this story is the trust that Dad had in Tom. It was almost a fatal trust. Call it naïve or foolish, but despite the dangerous circumstances, my dad had so much faith in his cousin that he literally trusted him with his life.

We should obviously avoid putting so much faith in another person, but this innocent trust is what we should place in Christ. As Jesus said, "I tell you the truth, anyone who doesn't receive the Kingdom of God like a child will never enter it" (Luke 18:17 NLT). What is so important about receiving God and His Kingdom like a child? I think there is an innocence of trust in our early years. A child's natural inclination is to trust first, and this trust is pure and genuine. There's no figuring out the angles, questioning of motives, or deciphering of agendas. Once that trust has been broken or damaged, the heart becomes a little more hardened—a little more wary and less trusting.

As we get older, this innocent trust is tempered with doubt and suspicion. We even develop some countermeasures such as shrewdness, cunning, and perhaps even a few of our own methods of deception and white lie spin. It's difficult to openly trust again when we've been hurt or burned, so in response we spend years building our own defenses. We've all been betrayed in a relationship or perhaps a business deal. The closer the other person is to you, the more painful it is. So we set up protective measures. We build walls. In many cases, we take these protective measures into our relationship with God. We can be respectful. I mean He *is* God. However, what's the point of building a fort if you're going to exist outside the walls? How can we put our full trust in God and just open ourselves up with complete vulnerability?

One defensive approach many of us take is that when we pray, we "bargain" with God—engage in quid pro quo arrangements such as, "I'll do this or give up this, Lord, if You'll do this for me." Ever done that? Then we sometimes use that to justify excluding God from our decision-making if a situation didn't go how we wanted. We rationalize: *I asked God for help in this area of my life (based on my terms and conditions) and He didn't come through for me so I'm now going to handle this on my own.* It doesn't work that way or it certainly will not work out well that way. God *can* be fully trusted. He made us and loves us beyond our comprehension and yes, He also *knows* and *desires* what is best for us.

He also knows everything about us including our thoughts and desires. We cannot hide anything. He *is* God. It's not as if you can surprise or shock Him. He'll never say, "Gee, I didn't know that," or "You know, I wish you hadn't told me that, because now I must summon my angels to inflict punishment on you." He knows all and He wants you to come to Him with everything—the good, the bad, and the ugly. No matter what you share with Him, He is always consistent with His response. He gives you love and lots of it!

God desires a loving relationship with us, and we are to trust Him with our whole heart and lean or depend not on our own understanding (Prov. 3:5). It is that childlike faith, that trusting and humble heart that pleases God. "Therefore, whoever humbles himself like this child is the greatest in the Kingdom of Heaven," Jesus told his disciples (Matt. 18:4 NIV).

Proverbs 3:6 goes on to say, "In all your ways acknowledge Him. And He will make your paths straight." The word "acknowledge" is a little weak in today's culture. It truly means to be focused on Him, or—as another translation puts it—"to seek His will in all that you do." He will make our paths straight or our path clear in our mind on where we are to go.

What a great promise. If we follow it, have a humble heart, and trust completely in the Lord, not only will we be considered "great" in the Kingdom of Heaven, but figuratively, God will keep us out of deep water and free us if we get stuck in the mud.

16. A Grandmother's Love

Doug Hanson

During a fall visit to an orphanage in Dornesti, Romania in 2000, I had been asked by fellow missionary, Ruben Popet to join him on a short ride in a station wagon to the Dornesti train station on the other side of the Suceava River to meet one of the orphans' grandmothers. She was coming by train to visit her granddaughter Nicoleta for the day, and the mile-long walk would be too much for her, especially since she often would bring gifts for Nicoleta and the children.

She had already arrived when we got to the train station. She was dressed in typical Romanian garb with a black skirt, a number of layered blouses, a sweater, and a dark brown scarf. The weather had cooled by late September, and she was ready for a sudden cold blast from northern Ukraine. Dornesti is only five miles from the Russian border.

With Nicoleta's grandmother were two large plaid bags loaded with fresh apples. No doubt, she had handpicked these from random trees across the area just before the trip. During the fall, it is most common to see families and individuals carrying long sticks to knock down free apples from the many trees that dot the landscape. How she was able to tote these heavy bags onto and off of the train was a miracle in itself. Both Ruben and I grabbed a bag, headed for the station wagon, and loaded her up for the short trip to the orphanage.

As we backed up into the orphanage's food-service dock, all the children came running. They seemed to have a sixth sense of when guests would be coming, particularly if the guests had gifts. We lifted the bags onto the dock and poured the hundreds of apples onto the concrete floor. The kids each got to have one, and the rest were sorted for pies, jams, and jellies. There was great laughter and appreciation for her thoughtfulness. Nicoleta was among the greeters, and her beautiful dark, Gypsy skin and black hair set off her smile like a picture. She was very glad to see someone from her immediate family.

Romanians consider children to be orphans if only one of their parents is missing or deceased. During the Communist years, most of the children were abandoned at birth, or several months afterwards, when their parents either determined that they could not feed them or when their patience with a hungry, crying child had vanished. Nicoleta was one of those children, and her grandmother was not able to care for her though she still had the love and presence to keep the relationship intact.

During the late morning, Nicoleta and her grandmother chatted and walked the orphanage grounds. They both had a lot of catching up to do. They enjoyed lunch together in the pine-paneled dining room, most probably soup, bread, and porridge. Her grandmother would stay through the early afternoon.

Meanwhile, after lunch, I had moved outside for some afternoon photographs. During the day, nomadic shepherds would come through the Suceava River banks with their huge flocks and patiently move with their dogs as their flock fed on the lush grass. Shepherds would stay with their flocks around the clock, seven days a week. In their native dress and with their crooks, they were quite a photo op.

It was while photographing one such shepherd that I glanced up behind the soccer field and noticed Nicoleta's grandmother walking along the railroad tracks on her way to the train station for her return trip home. She had traded apples for rolls of carpet and was laboriously carrying the two bags filled to overflowing with pieces of wool carpet. She was bent under the weight, and for a person of her age, she was making a super-human effort to keep moving.

I tucked my camera inside my jacket, zipped it over the lens for protection, and began to run around the perimeter of the soccer field to the train tracks. I knew the route to the tracks and across the Suceava River; it was the route we took every morning with the kids to their school. It was a good run to the tracks, about two U.S. city blocks. Once I arrived at the tracks, the route grew more level, but it was still difficult because of the discarded ballast and old concrete ties from the Communist era. I couldn't see Nicoleta's grandmother as I reached the edge of the bridge. Supposing that she was farther ahead of me and over the crest of the bridge, I ran faster, only to see a black object crumpled at the other end of the bridge, lying in the rail bed. Her carpetbags were strewn out with rolls everywhere. She was not moving.

My heart began to pound as I approached her. She was moaning and obviously injured. I heard the rumbling of a CRT switch engine as it appeared around a curve and rapidly approached us on the same track. I had to do something.

As an American visitor to the orphanage, the children enjoyed teaching me a few Romanian words. Fortunately for me, one of them was the word for *stop: opreste,* pronounced "o-presh-te." I stood in the rail bed in front of Nicoleta's grandmother, waving my arms frantically and shouting "Opreste! Opreste!"

I got the attention of the engineer, who brought the huge engine to a squeaky stop near her body. He was expressionless. He had nothing to say. His demeanor seemed to say, "Why are you doing this? You're wasting my time." I thanked him for stopping with another word I had learned from the kids—*multemesc*—and lifted the woman to her feet. Both of her knees were bleeding from the sudden contact with the sharp ballast, but I could tell that she was a strong woman and wanted to move on. She had a train to catch at the Dornesti station.

Sliding the carpet rolls back into the bags, I hoisted them up onto my shoulders, grabbed her black purse, and gave her my right arm to hold as we began our slow walk to the train station not yet visible ahead. How was I to know how injured she was? She could not tell me a word. She grimaced as she made her way along the side of the tracks. I knew we were getting closer to the station, as more tracks converged while we walked.

As we approached the station after a forty-minute walk, we could see a passenger train sitting on the tracks with the engine idling. I needed to get the grandmother to a place of rest, so I spotted one of the wooden benches, like a church pew, common to old train stations. She slumped into the seat exhausted.

A train conductor quickly approached her and asked her what her destination was. "Suceava?" he asked. Suceava is a large city 30 miles to the east near the Moldovan border, and the train must have been scheduled for there.

"Da," she said.

He asked her, "Billet?"

She fumbled through her purse and found her return ticket, handing it to the conductor.

He pointed to the ticket and then to her. "Your train," he said.

We walked to the nearest entry door for the coach in Class 2—the cheapest seats possible. There, the carriage's blue door was open, and the enormous steps awaited her to board. As she approached the first step, I could readily see that her injuries were too much to allow for an easy climb. There was no help from the conductor standing nearby, so I gently placed my two hands under her bottom and with one motion, pushed and lifted her onto the platform. I grabbed the two bags and placed them on the platform beside her.

The conductor blew a shrill whistle, one long blast. The train began to move and pull out of the station. The grandmother looked at me, patted her heart twice, and blew me a kiss as she rolled away. I was emotionally spent and broke down in tears.

In fact, I cried all the way back to the orphanage as I walked along the train tracks and across the bridge. I was so amazed at how God would use me, a visitor who did not know the language in this small village halfway around the world, to assist this loving grandmother who wanted to make a difference in her granddaughter's life and home. At the same time, He would stop not one but two trains in the process to show His grace to us both.

17. The Dash

Tom McAllister

One of the most powerful tools in the business world is the effective use of project management. Standard operating procedures adequately handle the business while it is in a steady state. However, any initiative, expansion, or improvement objective is best achieved through the use of "Best Practice" project management techniques.

The first step in defining a project is to define your goals by creating an accurate mission statement. Then you develop a "To Be" or Future State. Then next step, (which should be a given), is to describe your "As Is" or Current State. Then you design and build the best road map or migration path to go from where you are (Current State) to where you want to be (Future State).

Properly defining your Future State is critical. Without an accurately described future or end state, you never know when you get there or, even worse, you don't know if you're going in the right direction. You wouldn't get in your car and then have someone ask you where you are going, only to reply, "I don't know" (unless you're having one of those "senior moments").

Our lives here on earth are not that complicated. We all have the same end state. At some point we will give that bucket one final kick, the music will stop, the lights will go out, and the party will be over.

My first job was working for the city of the mighty metropolis of Graham, North Carolina, mowing graveyards and digging graves. Though it was a dead business, I dug it. Besides, everyone was dying to go there. Mowing cemeteries was a great leadership opportunity because on my first day, I already had lots of people under me. None of them would listen, though; I guess that's why they eventually let me go, as I just couldn't cut it. (All right, I'm done. I was just having too much pun.)

During my "mowings," it was interesting to see the different types of tombstones. There were old ones and new ones, big, elegant ones, and small, simple ones. Many had quotes and elaborate sayings, others were just plain, but they all had one thing in common. Besides the name, they had a date of birth and a date of death with a little dash in between.

In that little dash was their entire life. It contained all their efforts, hopes, and dreams whether they were realized or not. The sum total of their earthly life—all they ever did was contained in that one insignificant symbol.

That seems a bit understated, doesn't it? As we go through life in the ironic dichotomy of simultaneously living and dying, is the sum of our accomplishments simply remembered by a short, horizontal line?

As the sappy soap opera saying states, "Like sands through the hour glass, so are the days of our lives." So how's the sand passing for you? Is your life a beach, or is it more like 50-grit sandpaper? How are you doing your dash?

If we convert our life into a project plan, then we need to have a well-defined Future State. Life is a journey best traveled with a destination in mind. Knowing where you are going and the best way to get there is the optimal method for doing your dash and doing it well. Along the way, we should go with the Army slogan and be all that we can be.

But wait; there's more. No, it's not a free bamboo steamer or a Ginsu knife. It's great news. This is especially true if, so far, your dash isn't doing so hot. When the lights go out on your earthly life, it ain't over.

There's another dash! This dash starts at the date of your death, and it goes on forever. This is the real Future State.

This Future State is the one we must get right. It's your final dash. The proportions are correct as well. Our first dash is but a blip—the second is a line to infinity. You can screw up your first dash beyond all human comprehension, yet in a heartfelt instant get realigned and ensure your second dash is completely right. This is not the recommended strategy, of course, but that's incredible hope. As long as you are alive, there is no Current State too terrible that cannot be corrected. Accepting Christ as Lord of your life guarantees you the right Future State.

The author of the book of Hebrews stated it very succinctly: "And inasmuch as it is appointed for men to die once and after this comes judgment" (Heb. 9:27 NASB). Someday we all will have to give an account of how we lived—how we did our dash. If somewhere along the way in our first dash, we accepted Jesus Christ as our Lord and Savior, then our second dash is cash, and it's going to be a bash. No matter how good or bad the first dash went, this one will be awesome beyond words. You will certainly dig it. If you do not put your trust in Christ, then your dash is trash, and well, that's not a place you should be dying to go.

Don't wait to get straight your Future State. To delay is truly grave danger. Do the dash right by doing it with Christ. Then you will be in line for a great reward. For on that final Day of Judgment, our Lord will ascribe these words to your dash in life: "Well done, good and faithful servant. Come and share your Master's happiness." What a line! That is the dash of excellence—the awesome and infinite dash of eternal life!

18. Who's on First?

Tom McAllister

Our family has a wonderful tradition. Despite being scattered across four states, we all pick a weekend in December when we return to our original homestead and celebrate Christmas together. Each year we have a friendly, family feud in a football game between the kids and the adults, we go see a movie together, and in an all-hands-on-deck effort, we work together to prepare the Christmas Eve meal, which stresses Mom a bit, having so many in the kitchen. It's always an enjoyable time, and yes, we do it because we want to, but it happens because we make it a priority.

A recent family tradition, if you can call it that, was initiated by my older brother; he was the first one in the family lineage to make Eagle Scout. He led the way, and I, being the younger brother, followed suit. Now, all four of my nephews have achieved the rank of Eagle Scout, and my niece received her Gold Award, which is the highest rank in the Girl Scouts.

I cannot compliment enough the benefits I received in Scouting and the principles it taught me in building strong character traits with which to guide my life. A critical component is having good leaders, and I personally was blessed with having two who were outstanding. The twelve points of the Scout Law are timeless in their application. A

Scout is trustworthy, loyal, helpful, friendly, courteous, kind, obedient, cheerful, thrifty, brave, clean, and reverent. These are as valuable today as they were when the Boy Scouts started in 1910. If you are seeking a set of character-based building blocks, then these are a great baseline. [Sadly, the Boy Scouts' recent change to its membership policy now threatens to compromise its own oath to be morally straight. The Boy Scouts are in desperate need of prayer.]

Building character is like constructing a building. You need a firm foundation, and it is paramount to ensure that this base is laid correctly. When constructing a building, there is one block or stone that is more important than all the others are—the cornerstone. It is the first stone placed in the foundation, and all other stones are laid based on the position of the cornerstone.

If you're more of the interior decorator type, then use wallpaper as the analogy. When putting up wallpaper, which is a great project for young couples willing to test the strength of their marriage, the first piece is the most important because each piece placed after it is positioned based on the alignment of the first piece. If the first piece is laid incorrectly, then by the time you get around the room, you'll have a geometric mess. Then you may hear, "Uh, honey, why don't we just paint the room?"

A cornerstone also exists when it comes to instilling values and building character. Of all your priorities, principles, and values, there is one that is the most important—the one that supersedes all the rest. Everyone has a cornerstone. What is yours? What's the most important thing in your life? What should it be?

If you don't know what the most important thing in your life is, you need to pause for a moment and figure it out. This is your calibration point. This should be front and center in your brain and in your heart. The value to you of everything else in this world is based on what you have as your cornerstone. If you choose the wrong cornerstone, or your cornerstone is improperly placed, then your whole building will be out of alignment. If left unrepaired, then your building won't pass code; it will be condemned and torn down. That's not a good thing.

In the Gospel of Matthew, Jesus told a parable about a landowner and his vineyard (Matt. 21:33–41) that described the coming ruin of the Jewish nation because they rejected His teachings. The parable also explained how the Gentiles would be blessed for receiving Christ. In verses 42–43, Matthew writes:

> Then Jesus asked them, "Didn't you ever read this in the Scriptures? The stone that the builders rejected has now become the cornerstone. This is the LORD's doing, and it is wonderful to see. I tell you, the Kingdom of God will be taken away from you and given to a nation that will produce the proper fruit" (NLT).

The United States, which incorporated Jesus as "our Lord"[1] in its Constitution, has been an incredibly fruitful branch on the vine of Jesus. We declared that God, not our government, has given humankind certain inalienable rights to life, liberty, and the pursuit of happiness. Freedom is our nation's most cherished gift. The greatest freedom is freedom from sin, which can only be obtained through faith in Jesus Christ. As our country has drifted away from this precept, our productivity has declined, and our stature in the world has diminished.

We have choices. Jesus also addressed this cornerstone of choice and dilemma in His Sermon on the Mount (Matt. 6:24 ISV): "No one can serve two masters, because either he will hate one and love the other, or be loyal to one and despise the other. You cannot serve God and riches!" God knows the human heart (He designed it). Today, few people kneel and worship idols of wood and stone, but many idolize things of this world, such as personal wealth, power, and fame, more than they worship God. The human heart cannot be duplicitous in its loyalty. When it comes to having a number one, there can be only one.

That number one must be God.

He built us that way. We are created in His image to be aligned to His purpose. If we don't have Christ as our cornerstone, our "building" is misaligned. In the end, we won't pass code. Like a house built on sand, our building will not survive when the rain and winds come, but will fall in a great crash (Matt. 7:27). Jesus calls such a builder "foolish." However, if we have Christ as our cornerstone, and if we hear His words and put them into practice, we are "like a wise man who built his house on the rock. The rain came down, the streams rose, and the winds blew and beat against that house; yet it did not fall, because it had its foundation on the rock" (Matt. 7:24–25 NIV).

We must start first with Christ. He is the Rock on which we stand. With Christ as our cornerstone, we have a building of character that can withstand any storm. This applies to daily living as well: "Seek first His kingdom and His righteousness, and all these things [that you need] will be given to you as well" (Matt. 6:33). Like setting our watch to make sure that we are on time and in synch with the daily activities of the world, we need to set our spiritual compass to God. He needs to be first and the guiding force in all that we do.

There are many important things in our lives. We have our bills to pay, family to support, relationships to maintain, work to do, food to buy, healthcare needs, and all the events big and small that fight for our attention. God knows our needs. He promises that He will provide for us. If we have Christ as our cornerstone, if we make Him a priority, and if we seek first daily His kingdom in all that we do, then all that we need will be added or provided unto us.

It's a great promise. In these stressful times, it offers both hope and peace of mind. There's a simple saying: "No Christ. No peace. Know Christ. Know peace."

19. The Confusion that Confuses Me

Rick Saltzer

The image of a Christmas tree on the front page of that morning's *USA TODAY* yanked my attention from the maddening scent of the coffee counter to the colorful headlines of the newsstand. I instinctively wondered what politically correct Christmas news could possibly dominate above-the-fold space in "The Nation's Newspaper." Perhaps, it was a nicely timed fluff piece designed to distract reader attention from the high unemployment and economic woes. Alas, in a moment of caffeine-deprived weakness, I allowed my curiosity to overwhelm my sensibility, and I shamefacedly purchased a media product. I then quickly shuffled out of the store with my head down, bitterly chiding myself for consciously donating a buck to the liberal press.

I settled into the comforts of my front seat to wearily peruse what I expected to be the usual condescending, secular diatribe on the trivialities of "the winter holiday season." Surprisingly, the story actually had nothing to do with Christmas per se; however, it did provide some valuable, albeit alarming, insights into the composition of America's contemporary church via a recently concluded Pew research survey. To me, the real kick in the head was the inexplicable new perspective that groups of "Christians" and their leaders have begun to take on Christianity. Some of the key findings of the study detailed in the article were:

- Roughly two-thirds of U.S. adults, including many professed Protestants and Catholics, have begun to adopt elements of Eastern faiths and New Age thinking.
- Adherence to one clear faith is diminishing, and mixing/matching beliefs and practices is now becoming the new norm of worship. One researcher opined that the findings indicated a heightened degree of spiritual and religious openness, rather than a lack of seriousness.
- A majority of Americans have changed their religion one or more times, with most citing unmet spiritual needs or a change in their religious or moral beliefs.
- Some 92 percent believe in "God"; however, 70 percent maintained that different faiths can lead to eternal life and also felt that there were several ways to interpret the teachings of their religion.

The data seemed to indicate one clear conclusion on the status of faith in America: "rampant confusion"—the phrase used by one particular Christian leader quoted in the article to describe the revelations of the Pew research.

Ugh! Satan, the father of doubt and confusion, had apparently done his work well. Most adults probably would have agreed that the spiritual and moral Christian underpinnings of this nation have been eroding for a while, but the size of these numbers was scary. Suddenly, my twisting stomach and contorting brain convinced me to dump out the rest of my coffee and remove my tongue from my cheek while I fretted over that singular phrase: "rampant confusion."

As I sat there brandishing a coffee-stained newspaper for an hour or so, two quotes that dealt with the concept of confusion kept banging together in my head. Ironically, Ayn Rand, a well-known atheist, had written, "The hardest thing to explain is the glaringly evident which everybody had decided not to see"—sort of a one-line equivalent of *The Emperor's New Clothes*. Secondly, John MacArthur, the prominent Christian pastor and leader, had observed that the single biggest problem facing Christianity was "the terrible decline in Bible literacy."

The confluence of these two thoughts kept dragging me to the same conclusion: The confusion in Christianity depicted in the research and the subsequent article was either caused by not knowing the Truth (ignorance), or, worse yet, knowing the Truth but lacking the fortitude to accept or declare it. I confess I found myself confused by all the confusion.

For those confused Christians, a thorough reading of John's gospel should answer every question. Jesus Christ repeatedly and clearly stated His identity and His purpose. He clearly and repeatedly stated that He was the only way to eternal life, and explained how believers were to behave in their earthly lives. He clearly and repeatedly explained the eternal consequences of not accepting Him as Lord and Savior. He did not provide any other options, alternatives, or Plan Bs for us to contemplate. What was so confusing about that? Consider:

How many ways are there to eternal life? See John 14:6.

Must a Christian be born again? See John 3:3, 7.

What is eternal destiny of believers/unbelievers? See John 3:15–21, 6:40, 8:24.

Who is our "father" if we have not accepted Christ (i.e., other "religions")? See John 8:37–47.

Did Christ bring a new religion, a new belief-system, some new ideas, or the Truth? See John 1:17, 4:24, 8:31–32, 14:6, 18:37.

Again I asked myself, what could have been so confusing about these passages to a Bible reader? Or was it that *confusion* was, in fact, being confused with *rejection*? Was the Truth truly obvious in the Bible, and people didn't recognize or understand it (MacArthur's assessment)?

Or was it more accurate to say that the Truth was plainly revealed, but not acknowledged and accepted, as in The Emperor's New Clothes—something that, as Rand put it, was glaringly evident, but willingly overlooked?

After two hours of noodling over all these questions and attempting to sort through all the confusion, I was left with a basic answer that seemed to resolve the issues raised by the data above: Jesus Christ is Truth, and personal acceptance of and belief in the Truth results in eternal life for the believer. Any beliefs, faiths, religions, and so on, that are not of the Truth (John 8:37–47, 14:6) are untrue and, therefore, false. Believers in that which is false will be eternally condemned. These are God's rules, not mine, and they are plainly written. God's rules are not politically correct. We won't have any rights, and we won't get a phone call or a lawyer. There'll be no protests, demonstrations, or boycotts. Follow the rules and we spend eternity in Heaven—reject them and spend eternity in Hell.

I was finally shaken out of my trance by the sound of my jingling cell phone. I let it ring while I reflected on the unexpected turn my morning had taken, all because I had broken my own vow not to subsidize the left-leaning media. I chalked it up to another example of the price one pays for lapses in self-discipline, although a part of me suspected that this was one of the most productive mornings I had ever experienced.

Now it was time for that coffee.

20. My Lord

Jeff McAdams

He came to earth one glorious night
The Morning Star aglow;
And gloried in the Father's will,
To Calvary He did go.

He did not have to die for me,
Of this I fully know;
But yet He died upon the cross,
So many years ago.

And though He died He lives again,
To Heaven He did go;
But soon He'll come in glory bright,
To crush the evil foe.

I've sinned against a Holy God,
And fallen oh so low;
And though the wage of sin is death,
His mercy doth He show.

My sins are covered by His blood,
His grace doth overflow;
My Lord and Savior Jesus Christ,
Oh how He loves me so.

21. Truth or Consequences, Part II

Tom McAllister

Many people remember the comedian Flip Wilson and his famous saying, "The devil made me do it." Although the devil doesn't make anyone do anything, he certainly encourages misbehavior. Satan is a defeated foe, as Christ kicked his pointy tail at Calvary. His fate is sealed, and he is doomed to spend all eternity in the Lake of Fire. However, until that time comes, he is still a powerful adversary, and his whole purpose in life is to exalt himself and to thwart the purposes of God.

God is all-knowing, and therefore possesses total Truth. Satan is opposed to God and therefore is opposed to the Truth. He is the father of lies, and there is no truth in him (John 8:44). Since everything about him is a lie, he has nothing to offer but a marketing plan devoted to deception. Paul even warns us that Satan sometimes disguises himself as an angel of light (2 Cor. 11:14). Knowing that we do not have the whole truth, "for presently we see in a mirror dimly" (1 Cor. 13:12), he needs to bend the truth just enough to lead people astray. Unfortunately, he is very skilled at this.

The devil has made great progress over the last fifty years. Here in the United States—the largest Christian nation in the world—his efforts have gotten prayer out of schools, increased our tendency and tolerance for violence, made fornication and abortion mainstream, greatly increased the rates of divorce and unwed pregnancies, and moved homosexual behavior way out of the closet. Breaking down or perverting the family unit is Satan's strategic goal, as it promotes dysfunctional behavior in future generations.

Here are just two of his many recent marketing campaigns that, when combined, may fool multitudes. When you analyze it, you'll have to admit that it's a clever plan. In military terms, it combines a decoy frontal assault that may capture only a few of us, but which will, if successful, drive a majority of us toward what seems to be a safer alternative, but is really an ambush.

The direct frontal attack consists of the recent ad campaigns run by various atheist organizations. The devil considers atheists as useful idiots. Though they don't even believe in Satan's existence, these people are nonetheless important accomplices in his efforts to rule the world. Some of these ads ran during the Christmas holiday stating that there is *no* "reason for the season" and that we should just be good for goodness' sake. In Europe, another effort launched an ad that said, "There's probably no God. Now stop worrying and enjoy your life."[1]

Let's contemplate the wisdom of this last slogan, for it is fraught with foolishness and deception. The first sentence paraphrases a Bible verse. Psalm 14:1b actually states, "There is no God." Of course, this is a perfect example of taking a line out of context, because the whole verse states, "For the fool says in his heart, 'There is no God.' They are corrupt, their deeds are vile; there is no one who does good." If you want to be a fool, or a useful idiot for the devil, then don't believe in God.

Second, those who have accepted Jesus Christ aren't worried about their salvation. Only the unsaved should worry. If they sense it, then it is the Holy Spirit trying to trouble their consciences to turn them from their destiny of death. For there are none righteous, not even one—all have sinned, and the wages of sin is death (Rom. 3:10, 23; 6:23).

Notice also that saying there's "probably" no God is not as shocking as the blunt statement that there is no God. All Satan needs is a response of, "You're probably right." Lulling a person into apathy about God is just as big a success for the devil as causing someone to be in direct opposition to God. One must proactively choose God. Not deciding or caring is the same as voting "No."

Finally, even the logic is faulty. If there was no eternal life, then at death the lights go out, the party's over, and everybody loses equally. We all die and become dust. However, if there is an eternal life provided by God, then those who put their trust in Him will win and receive an eternal reward, while those who don't will lose big time. So even using the ad's logic, if you bet on God, even with their suggested improbable odds, you still may win. If you don't, you'll *always* lose.

The second marketing campaign of deception is far more subtle and dangerous. If people recoil from the notion that there's probably no God, then where will they go? Perhaps they'll head in the general direction of believing in a Creator. If they are not too particular about the direction they go, they may develop some form of believing in God in a generic, politically correct sense and would thus consider seeking the Kingdom of God to be a reasonably worthy pursuit. If they follow mainstream culture, this somewhat rudderless drift toward God could actually take them into currents where they should not travel.

These mainstream "dangerous" waters are found in the New Age movement and a growing post-modern philosophy within certain segments of the church itself. This undertow emphasizes the need to address major social issues, such as feeding the poor, preventing disease such as the spread of AIDS, and tackling environmental concerns ranging from pollution to global climate change. These are all worthwhile issues to pursue, and there is much synergy in the fact that virtually all forms of religion can embrace them. These movements promote the concept of creating the Kingdom of God here on earth by initiating efforts to improve the quality of life for all of humankind. Once again, these are noble goals, but the focus becomes more of a social agenda rather than a salvation agenda.[2] It's a hedge bet. For those of you who felt a twinge of worry or angst when you read, "There's probably no God," these positive social efforts probably seem soothing to the soul. If so, please be careful. Satan is singing you a lullaby.

The Great Commission for all Christians is to preach the Gospel to all nations about the saving grace of Jesus Christ. This is the foremost objective, and all other pursuits pale in comparison. Jesus Christ is the antidote to our sinful nature, and only He gives us the cure. He is the hope of glory. To reject Christ is to reject the One Who sent Him, which is God the Father. Contemplate the extreme for a moment. If it were possible to enable every human on earth to have enough food and supplies to be healthy and safe from harm, yet not have Christ, then all would be lost. As we've stated in previous ROI analysis, it would be better to suffer every day on earth with Christ than have the whole world and be without Him, for what profit is there to gain the whole world and lose your soul?

Any effort without Christ is without merit. As Jesus said about Himself, "I am the vine, you are the branches; he who abides in Me and I in him, he bears much fruit, for apart from Me you can do nothing" (John 15:5 NASB). Without Christ, we can do nothing. Satan's deception is to pump up our pride about what *we* can do by leading humankind to pursue a noble goal without the most noble of all—Jesus Christ. Christ is the source of all good fruit. Unless people realize this, they will be deceived.

A general movement with a positive social agenda has mass appeal. All can agree on a message of hope and help, and it could easily lead to a unifying and perhaps universal "religion" whose central tenets are simply, "love one another" and "be good caretakers of our planet." The whole concept seems like a winner, doesn't it? What if the whole world could embrace such a concept and support such a movement? Wouldn't it make all our lives better?

It's a great plan of future deception. Like a wrestling or jujitsu move where you use your opponent's own momentum or inertia to flip him over, Satan can use such a positive "movement" to flip people away from the true God and His plan of salvation through His Son. Think about all the world's religions slowly unifying in thought and heading toward this common goal of ending poverty, starvation, disease, and environmental destruction. It's a worthwhile objective, and it complies with political correctness. Such a movement could gain significant momentum in a hurry, especially if the world economy is in trouble. People would want to create solutions and do their part. The more people gravitated toward and joined this global quasi-religious movement, the more momentum it would have. On the surface, it would have a very positive benefit for the world, but here's how Satan would take this positive movement and flip it. Imagine Christians standing up and claiming that the root of our problems is sin, and that we must accept Christ and Christ alone as our Savior. Would such claims be considered inclusive or divisive? Would Christians be welcomed or ostracized?

Satan will gladly give ground to a positive social agenda if he can minimize or eliminate the emphasis on Christ.[3] It was Christ Who defeated him on the cross. Now, he will try to use a positive movement with good intentions to lead people away from the only source of their salvation. A sound social agenda of aiding the poor and the sick, loving your neighbor, and being good stewards of our planet is a wonderful objective. This is only the second half of the greatest commandment. The first half is to love God with all your heart, mind, body, soul, and strength. We cannot love God if we ignore His Son. This wonderful agenda should be done through the power of Christ, not in place of Him.

In his letter to the Colossians, Paul stated the proper attitude and approach:

Our goal is to live a life worthy of the Lord and to please Him in every way: bearing fruit in every good work, growing in the knowledge of God, being strengthened with all power according to His glorious might so that you may have great endurance and patience, and joyfully giving thanks to the Father, Who has qualified you to share in the inheritance of the saints in the kingdom of light. For He has rescued us from the dominion of darkness and brought us into the kingdom of the Son He loves, in Whom we have redemption, the forgiveness of sins. He is the image of the invisible God, the Firstborn over all creation. For by Him all things were created: things in Heaven and on earth, visible and invisible, whether thrones or powers or rulers or authorities; all things were created by Him and for Him. He is before all things, and in Him all things hold together (Col. 1:10–17 NIV).

Christ holds the world together. He holds this whole universe together. Any effort or objective, no matter how wonderful in appearance, is worthless without Christ. Do not be deceived. Whatever we do, we should be centered on Him. Jesus Christ is our All in All. He is the Way, the Truth, and the Life. Believe in that truth, and it will set you free. The consequences of not believing and accepting this truth are absolutely devilish.

22. Answering the Call

Kathryn Mae Rogers

When I was eleven years old, I was saved at Sardis Baptist Church and baptized in Lake Lanier. To bring me to this milestone in life were Christian parents who taught me many things in life including many things about Jesus Christ.

Moving forward to the year 2002, I was looking at turning fifty years old in three years. My question to myself was, *What is it I want out of the rest of my life?*

I started to think and to pray. It is time to get back to me. I needed to start finding ways to fill my time because my son, Jonathan, would soon be driving and wouldn't need me as much. I wanted and continue to want to be the best parent possible and encourage his independence. I had a lot on my mind and I wasn't happy with the way my life was turning out.

The company I worked for wanted me to attend a Dale Carnegie course. I asked my friend, Steve, to start praying that someone else would be going so I could at least have someone I knew to hang out with. He told me he was going. That was a wonderful relief. He is such a nice person, which would make this fun.

During the time of attending the Dale Carnegie class, Steve and I found we could talk about anything. At this point Steve and I became very close friends. As the Dale Carnegie class came to a close, I started hearing about the Stephen Ministry, which trained laypeople to be listeners. Steve showed me the website; I started gathering information. The time came to sign up for the Stephen Ministry class. I was excited and afraid at the same time.

In January 2003 the Stephen Ministry classes began. I clung to every word being taught and could not wait for Thursday nights.

A prayer was said in class for two Stephen Leaders to step forward. My chest was pounding. *Me? Surely not me.* The next day I called a current Stephen Leader. I asked him if we could talk that day. I told him of my feelings and requested that he try to talk me out of this.

I told the Stephen Minister Leader, "Not me—I'm too shy."

The leader told me, "If God is calling, you had better answer." He said that the church would pay the expenses, and all I needed to do was give a week of my time.

I thought, *A week of my time…for me? Is this how I am going to find me again?*

Commissioning Sunday was approaching. Leaving for Leadership training was coming, and I would be leaving soon. This is not exactly what I had been looking as way to keep busy. But I knew God was calling, and I needed to answer.

I invited several friends to Commissioning Services, including Steve. I really wanted him to come; we had become very special friends. I also knew he was praying hard for me. He was supportive in many ways, including encouraging me to become a Stephen Leader. By the end of the Leader training and my return home, I knew I needed some changes in my life.

Steve and I had talked every day, and I knew he was praying for me. I had also realized that he was in love with me, and I with him. I asked myself, *Why am I in love with this wonderful man at this stage in life? So many things must happen for us to even think about anything beyond a friendship.* I had prayed for something to fill my time in the evenings, but being in love and the thoughts of marriage were not on my list.

I started praying again and started to try and make sense of all of this, often asking myself, *Why me?* We had learned in Stephen Ministry about how to accomplish our goals. We also learned how sometimes God's hand worked through other people, and how all things occurred in God's time.

Okay, I thought, *I am going to be a leader, so I need to put all these skills I have learned to the test.*

Process takes patience, and patience is not one of my strong points, but I was determined to give it a try. I prayed that I would know what to do and would know it was the right thing.

I gave God a laundry list of things that I felt needed to happen; selling two houses, buying a house, as well as many more things. *Okay, I am going to see. This process thing is supposed to work.*

Slowly things began to happen, and in time, everything I had asked for had happened. *Okay, this process thing does work.*

Steve began coming to First Baptist Church with me and soon felt the call to move his Church membership to First Baptist. Steve asked me to marry him after all of our individual goals were met. I was afraid of so many things. I started praying again. I felt secure enough in accepting his proposal after many hours of prayer. We announced our plans for marriage; the affirmation came from our friends, and so many blessings came that I knew God was in this. We started planning a wedding and a celebration. As plans were being made, I knew God had this plan for me and I was truly blessed.

The training and skills from Stephen Ministry was a contributor to my learning to listen to God and be obedient. God has blessed me with a partner who is beautiful inside and out.

I thought of Psalm 46:10: "Be still and know."

A little voice directed Steve and me to Kirkwood Baptist upon moving to St. Louis three years ago. The voice came from two of our precious friends at First Baptist Church, Gainesville, Georgia. Their words were, "If you must go, find Kirkwood Baptist Church." Their words kept repeating in my mind.

Kirkwood Baptist had been waiting for us as a church family, ready to receive us and love us; a church family to walk with us on our journey of life in St. Louis. Steve and I are blessed. The prayers of our church family have carried us many times in the past year. I thank them for that.

Soon after visiting Kirkwood and having a conversation with the pastor, I knew why we were in St. Louis. God was using Steve and me to bring Stephen Ministry to Kirkwood. It was an answer to Steve's prayer that I would find a way to use my Stephen Ministry Leader skills. God's unlimited amazing grace provided me with the time and energy to make a difference at Kirkwood, and I am humbled.

Kirkwood Baptist Church welcomed Steve and me and we are grateful. God led us here and we are blessed.

23. Payback

Tom McAllister

If you're a sports fan, one of the secular enjoyments of the Christmas season is the college football bowl games. These bowl games serve as a reward to those college teams that did well during the year. Though the over expansion of the bowl system has somewhat diluted that standard (teams that are just .500 can qualify), the process provides a greater benefit to a larger number of schools and their fans.

Among the many sponsors advertising during this timeframe is a large credit card company that promotes its reward system of embedding your desired photo on the credit card, having low interest rates, providing cash back, and/or awarding prizes and benefits just for being a member. Their slogan is, "What's in your wallet?" Another credit card company has a slogan, "Membership has its privileges." Both companies state that becoming a customer or member of their programs will open the door to lots of benefits and rewards that you otherwise would not have.

Did you know that God has a rewards program, too? It's true, and like the credit card companies, the rewards only apply to members. Fortunately, it doesn't have the prerequisite financial qualifications to become a member like the credit card companies demand. To become a member of God's rewards program requires no money, talent, status, or effort. It simply takes belief.

There are multiple membership clauses in the Bible: Acts 16:31a reads, "Believe in the Lord Jesus, and you will be saved"; Mark 16:16 reads, "Believe…and you will be saved"; Rom. 10:9 (NLT) reads, "If you confess with your mouth, 'Jesus is Lord,' and believe in your heart that God raised Him from the dead, you will be saved"; and, of course, perhaps the most famous, John 3:16 (NASB) says, "For God so loved the world, that He gave His only begotten Son, that whoever believes in Him shall not perish, but have eternal life."

Once you become a member, you are a member for life—everlasting life. You cannot be disqualified: "I give them eternal life, and they shall never perish; no one can snatch them out of My hand. My Father, Who has given them to Me, is greater than all; and no one is able to snatch them out of My Father's hand" (John 10:28–29 NIV).

Pretty cool, huh? Here's another commercial message—if you think you are in "good hands" with Allstate, then consider how safe you are in the hands of Jesus and the Father.

So how does this Heavenly rewards program work? We are evaluated by Christ: "For we must all appear before the judgment seat of Christ, that each one may receive what is due him for the things done while in the body, whether good or bad" (2 Cor. 5:10 NIV). It works based on our work as each will receive his own reward according to his own labor (1 Cor. 3:8). God is our cosmic CEO—He built this entire universe and all things in it are under His domain. As children of God, it's a family-owned business. We all work for Dad. At the end of this world He will have a wonderful awards banquet with His Son Jesus as Master of Ceremonies. Pretty righteous, huh?

Continuing with Paul's letter to the Corinthians, he gives a building analogy similar to building up reward points for your credit card. Every time you use your card you get points. Every time you use your talents for the Lord, you get points. (1 Cor. 3:9): "For we are God's fellow workers; you are God's field, God's building" and skipping to verse 11:

"For no one can lay any foundation other than the one already laid, which is Jesus Christ."

There's a reference to the membership clause again. The rewards program is based on the belief of Jesus Christ. Without that belief, you're not a member of the program, and any work performed is for nada, nil, nilo, zip, zilch, zero—no credit applied. It's the ultimate, "Sorry, Charlie" of Starkist tuna fame. Without Christ, your works are rejected.

So upon this critical foundation of Jesus Christ your membership program begins: "If any man builds on this foundation using gold, silver, costly stones, wood, hay or straw, his work will be shown for what it is, because the [Judgment] Day will bring it to light. It will be revealed with fire, and the fire will test the quality of each man's work. If what he has built survives, he will receive his reward" (1 Cor. 3:12–14 NIV).

How often have you heard that the quality of a product is based on the tools and materials that were used to make it? Well, in this scenario, you are the tool and the material is your attitude of heart. The actual accomplishment is less valuable than the attitude in which you performed it. If the work you performed is done with an attitude of selfless love, then it is purified through fire—notice gold, silver, and precious stones are refined through fire and made more brilliant. Wood, hay, straw, or actions performed with ulterior or selfish motives are consumed and destroyed. There is no cheese (or rewards) down these tunnels. "As they are, you will suffer loss, though you yourself will be saved" (1 Cor. 3:15 ESV). This is not a salvation thing—you get your membership from your belief in Jesus Christ and you are forever in the good hands of the Father and the Son—this cannot be taken away. This is a rewards program, and actions performed with improper motives, no matter how impressive, simply do not earn points.

Later in his letter (chapter 13), Paul gives the ideal motivation for all action—love. In fact, he states very clearly that any action—even great and impressive things such as chatting with angels ("Hey Gabriel,

115

how are the stars hangin'?") or predicting the future, feeding all the poor, knowing all sorts of mysteries, making huge personal sacrifices or moving mountains by pure faith—any action done without love is for naught.

Love is the essential ingredient in all action. When asked what the greatest commandment was, Jesus replied, "'Love the Lord your God with all your heart and with all your soul and with all your strength and with all your mind' and, 'Love your neighbor as yourself'" (Mark 12:30–31 NIV). If you want the Cliff Notes version of all the rules and regulations, all the "Thou shall" and "Thou shall nots" of the Bible, then this verse is it. And it has only one verb—love.

As the first sentence and key concept of Rick Warren's mega-selling book, *The Purpose Driven Life*, states, "It's not about you." It's about God as our Creator, CEO, and Father. This is His world, and He has a purpose for each and every one of us. For those who follow His program, there exists a Heavenly reward. "Let us not become weary in doing good, for at the proper time we will reap a harvest [your reward] if we do not give up" (Gal. 6:9 NIV). Invest your 401(k) program into the Kingdom of God. "Store your treasures in Heaven, where moths and rust cannot destroy, and thieves do not break in and steal" (Matt. 6:20 NLT). This is the wisest course of action.

Now, let's get back to the tasks at hand. Let us keep working and doing all things in love for it is not what's in your wallet, but what's in your heart that counts. Also remember that membership has its privileges, and in God's program those privileges that you have and the rewards that you earn last forever.

24. This is a Test

Tom McAllister

Stephen Ministry is a program where lay personnel (Blue Collar faith walkers) have been trained and are supervised in providing one-on-one care to individuals going through an emotionally difficult situation or crisis. A typical scenario is that the Stephen Minister will spend about an hour or more a week providing support with his or her "care receiver" in a spiritual walk together through the care receiver's season of difficulty.

I became a Stephen Minister about eight years ago. When I first signed up for the program, I really didn't know what to expect. Most of the training made logical sense until we got to the methodology. Here we were told that it was a process-oriented methodology, not a results-oriented methodology.

At that point I said, "Whoa! Hold it! Time out...We're here to help these people through their problems, right? Aren't we looking for good results? Let me help out as I'm a consultant. I'll explain to you how business world 'best practices' problem-solving works. First you define the problem you are facing. Then you assess your current situation. This is called the *As Is* or *Current State*. Then you envision where you want to be. This is your *To Be* or *Future State*. The final step is to develop a plan or roadmap of the set of tasks, milestones, and objectives necessary to get you from your Current State to your Future State. Then it's just, 'Get 'er done.'"

As I soon discovered, the Stephen Ministry is nothing like that.

The first thing you realize in Stephen Ministry is that you are just the helper; God is the Healer. You're just the vessel; you're just the conduit for His love, mercy, and grace to flow through you to meet the care-receiver's needs.

Learning this methodology has been one of the greatest blessings in my life. As a Stephen Minister, I have had the privilege of a front row seat watching the hand of God work in someone else's life. As Bob Uecker would say, "I'm up on the front row." Of course there was prayer and preparation before each weekly meeting, but once our sessions got into the groove, you could sense the Holy Spirit leading the interaction. It got to a point where I would just have the attitude of "Let's break out the popcorn and see what God is going to do next."

Loving and helping your care receiver is not about following a set of tasks or meeting a bunch of milestones and deliverables. It is simply having a listening ear, a compassionate heart, and taking your care-receivers' hands and helping them re-establish their grip into the hand of Jesus Christ. When you trust in the Lord with all your heart, and lean not on your own understanding (for that understanding can get real cloudy under very stressful situations), He will direct your path and He will get you through the valley that you are in.

Let's consider the big picture for a moment and apply these Stephen minister principles to our nation's current state of affairs. Today, you don't have to be a prophet to see the dark clouds out there on the horizon. They are already overhead. Our country is going through a difficult time right now and it probably will get worse—in some scenarios a lot worse. Our circumstances are a much deeper problem than just a financial crisis, high unemployment, and total lack of teamwork among government leaders. There is a spiritual battle going on for our nation's soul.

But we Christians should not cower in fear. In fact we should do the opposite and stand up, close ranks, put on the full armor of God, and get in the game. *Let's get ready to rumble!* We need to activate the entire spiritual militia across this great land and pray daily for our nation, look after our neighbors, and help out those in need. We should "bear one another's burdens and thereby fulfill the law of Christ" (Gal. 6:2 NASB).

There are forces within our nation that are either naively or intentionally leading us away from what makes America great. Our greatness comes from the fact that we are under God. However, we need to do more than think it or say it—we need to live it! Folks, we have an awesome God who loves us and wants to bless us! In the spirit of 2 Chronicles 7:14, "If we the people, who are called by His name, will humble ourselves, repent of our wicked ways, seek His face and go to the LORD in prayer, He will hear our prayer, pardon our sins, and restore our land." If we want God to fix the problem, then here *is* the solution. God will do what He says. We must rally our brethren in Christ, promote the Gospel, and get our nation in a position so that God can bless us. That position is on our knees in prayer.

God did not give us a spirit of fear. He gave us a spirit of power and of love, and love never fails. God never fails. If God is for us, then who cares who's against us? I'd be like a pick-up game of basketball where you and the devil are team captains: "Hey, I choose Jesus. Devil, you can take as many draft picks as you want." With Christ, we're already on the winning team. It's guaranteed! That's not just in the next life, but in this life right here, right now.

Knowing all that, however, doesn't make the road we're traveling on any less bumpy. The reason we call it a tough time is because it's tough. We all will go through trials and have tests in our lifetime. That's inevitable. Through God's Providence that we don't fully understand, some of us will face a much more difficult exam than others.

There are typically two distinct responses that we have when facing adversity. We either become better or bitter. Unfortunately, we seem to parallel the rules of the English language where it is "i" before "e," and our initial default response is that we become bitter. We ask, "Why me, Lord?" Then we wallow in replaying scenarios of what could have been instead of what currently is.

Like the English language however, there is an exception to the rule. It is "i" before "e" except when following C. When you follow C, when you follow Christ, it is "e" before "i." When faced with a difficult trial—you get better.

One of the most difficult tasks as a Christian is to heed the advice of James and "consider it all joy" when we face trials. It requires a lot of trust to grasp that what you are going through is glorifying God and increasing your capacity to produce good fruit. The apostle Peter encourages us to persevere:

> ...though you may have had to suffer grief through many trials. They have come so that your faith—of greater worth than gold, which perishes even though refined by fire—may be proved genuine and may result in praise, glory and honor when Jesus Christ is revealed" (1 Peter 1:6b–7 NIV).

Our Lord promises us that He will never leave us or forsake us. We can cast our burdens upon Him, and He will sustain us through whatever circumstance we face. That is a great comfort and gives us that peace of mind that passes all understanding even in the most difficult of storms. We must anchor our heart in that promise. When we do, we can go forward in whatever situation, confidently knowing that when we walk with the Lord, He will get us over every hill and through every valley that we face. We can do all things through Christ, Who strengthens us.

25. Lord of the Rings

Tom McAllister

How did we sports fans ever survive without instant replay? One could only guess the number of games where the outcome would have changed had the inclusion of this modern video technology been available. Many "purists" would argue against having instant replay as it slows down the game and interrupts the flow. There's also the psychological effect on the referees—do they try harder because they are now more scrutinized, or do they relax because they have replay as their backup?

No matter what your opinion of instant replay, you must admit that the goal is noble. It's not about appeasing the home crowd or increasing network ratings by keeping the game close, although many fans suspect this when a call doesn't go their way. The goal is to discover the truth—what truly happened on the play in question. Did the receiver have the ball, was the serve in or out, or did the clock run out before the shot? Inquiring minds want to know.

Seeking the truth is never a waste of time. Knowing the truth is a valuable asset. Understanding the truth opens doors to opportunity. Truth is the universal measuring stick for how we should evaluate our circumstances and make our decisions.

What is truth? Ironically, Pilate asked that very question to Jesus— the very One Who is Truth. He was looking at Truth and speaking to

Truth, and he didn't even know it. In this earthly life, we will never know the full truth about everything. That would require omniscience. Yet there is one truth that you should grab hold of and hang on to with all you have: Jesus Christ is Lord. He is God's Son, the Light of the world, the Savior of the world, and He is the Way (to act), the Truth (to believe), and the Life (to live). Everything else pales in comparison to this fundamental truth. It is the cornerstone of Christian faith. It is Truth.

You can debate the merits of sprinkling versus full immersion in baptism. You can ponder the mystery of communion—does Christ enter the bread and wine when the priest rings a bell (Catholic), enter it upon consumption (Lutheran), or are the bread and wine simply symbols to remind us of the body and blood of Christ (Baptist)? You can even quibble about where to draw the salvation line. It is by faith alone, yes, but faith without works is dead (or not legitimate faith). Therefore, should you move it an infinitesimal smidge toward some type of "work" that validates your faith? These are worthwhile topics to consider, but the most important thing is simply to accept Jesus Christ as Lord.

We can move a few hours forward from when Pilate spoke to Jesus to another man who spoke to Jesus. We don't know his name, only that he was a criminal and he was being crucified beside our Lord. We do know what he said, and we recognize that through God's amazing grace, he saw the Truth. In a humble confession of repentance, he said, "Lord, remember me when You come into Your kingdom" (Luke 23:42 AKJV). That's all it took. Jesus confirmed this when He replied, "I tell you the truth, today you will be with Me in paradise" (Luke 23:43 NIV).

There was no baptism. There was no breaking of bread and sharing of wine. There were no good deeds—it's a little difficult to accomplish anything when you're nailed to a cross. It was simply a genuine, heartfelt recognition and trust in the Lordship of Jesus.

So does this mean that we pause for a moment, say those nine words, and then go back to our regularly scheduled program already in progress? Of course it doesn't. Accepting Christ is a life-altering event. Following Christ is a lifelong journey of dedication. You pick up your cross daily and follow Him. This is not a punishment; this is a blessing, for His yoke is easy, and His burden is light. All who are heavy laden will find rest in Him. It's a journey of peace and true fulfillment. We serve Him out of honor and love. We worship Him and give glory to Him because He is fully entitled to it. Baptism is our public statement of our lifetime commitment to Christ. When we take communion, we reflect on His overwhelming sacrifice and His love and His grace that He bestows upon us. We do this in remembrance of Him.

When you accept Christ as your Savior, it's the commitment of a lifetime for a lifetime. It's also the obvious recognition that God knows best, and that He loves you infinitely more than anyone else does, and therefore His way and purpose for you is far better than any plan that you can conceive on your own. When you grasp the Big Picture, you recognize that though you live in this world, you are not of this world. Like those instant replay cameras, you gain a different perspective on what's going on; you gain a better insight into the truth. You view life differently. As you open your heart and surrender your will to Christ, your life merges with His will in such a way that you understand what the apostle Paul is saying when he writes, "I have been crucified with Christ; and it is no longer I who live, but Christ lives in me; and the life which I now live in the flesh I live by faith in the Son of God, who loved me and gave Himself up for me" (Gal.2:20 NASB).

In his book, *The Rest of the Gospel*, Dan Stone provides some excellent illustrations of this different perspective that Christians should have of this earthly life. It's like drawing a horizontal line. Above the line is the unseen, eternal world, and below the line is this temporal world. We live below the line, but our perspective should be from above the line. As Paul puts it in 2 Corinthians 4:18 (NIV), "So we fix our eyes not on what is seen, but on what is unseen. For what is seen is temporary, but what is unseen is eternal."

This is a difficult saying for left-brained people. It causes a cocking of the head, a furrowing of the brow, and a guttural utterance of Scooby Doo fame, "Harr-ur-ruuh?" How can we fix our eyes upon something that cannot be seen? How would we know that we're even looking at it? We do not use our physical eyes, but our spiritual eyes. This isn't some mystical "third eye" where you must meditate, chant, and burn incense to get it to open. It's a perspective of seeing things from God's eternal view.

As John Polkinhorne describes, it's like putting on God's spectacles behind your eyes. Circumstances viewed as challenges become opportunities. A difficult trial in our lives may produce suffering for us in the temporal world, but if we persevere, it gives glory to God. In the parable of the Good Samaritan, the victim of the robbers was an inconvenience to the priest and the Levite who passed him by. They each had some worldly objective or meeting to attend that could not be interrupted or delayed to help a wounded man. The Samaritan perceived the situation differently. He saw the man as an opportunity to serve and to help a person in need. This is what is meant by viewing life from a different set of priorities and a Christ-like frame of reference.

We live by faith, knowing that "faith is the confidence that what we hope for will actually happen; it gives us assurance about things we cannot see" (Heb. 11:1 NLT). It's the true perspective of the Kingdom of God. Knowing that Christ is living through us and that God is in control gives us rest and peace.

Another one of Stone's illustrations demonstrates the three aspects of the human persona. We have our physical part, our mental and emotional part (often called the psyche), and our spiritual part. Now think how this triad operates together. Try to picture three concentric rings. The outer ring is the physical. The next ring is the psyche, and the inner ring is the spiritual. Surrounding these three rings is the world or the environment in which we live.

Now, the vast majority of information comes into our physical being through the environment. It comes through our five senses. We see things, we hear things, and we smell, taste, and touch things. This input goes from our outer physical ring to the second ring, which is where our mental and emotional abilities reside. Here the information is processed. Once it has been evaluated, the information is typically sent back through the physical body in the form of a response—a physical action or facial expression, and/or a verbal retort. This happens thousands of times a day. What's your spirit doing during all of this? Sometimes that "inner voice" provides moral input. Most of the time, its "opinion" is never solicited.

When we accept Christ as our Savior, the Holy Spirit dwells within us and becomes connected with our spirit. In 1 Corinthians 6:17 (NASB), Paul writes, "But the one who joins himself to the Lord is *one spirit* with Him" (emphasis added). This is your source of strength and power.

Let's go back to the process described above. Input comes in through the senses. It goes to the mind or psyche. The next step is for the psyche to consult with the spirit, and the spirit (which is connected to the Holy Spirit), "advises" the psyche on how to direct the physical body to respond. This is how Christ lives through you.

Why does Paul advise us to "pray unceasingly" (1 Thess. 5:17) and to be "praying at all times in the Spirit" (Eph. 6:18)? First, it establishes our reliance on God. Secondly, it helps us to retrain our brain to point in the right direction. If we are in constant communication with God, the communication link between our mind and our spirit is open. We operate from a prayer-spirit-communication-consciousness state. The input from the world comes in through our senses; the mind then receives that input, consults with our spirit, which is linked to the Holy Spirit, and our spirit generates the proper response back through the mind to the body. This God-consciousness state enables us to see the world from the eternal perspective of the Kingdom of God.

Thus, if we could be placed in the parable of the Good Samaritan, we would not be so focused on ourselves—we would have that psyche-spirit communication—and thus we would decide that it would not be an inconvenience to help a person in dire need of assistance. In our God-conscious state, we would immediately recognize a brother in need, and feel blessed to be able to share God's love by giving him aid. It is the act of maintaining that God-conscious, spirit-psyche link of constant communication that is critical for allowing God's Spirit to direct us to respond to situations in the correct way.

Look at our Master, Jesus. We read in the Bible how our Lord Jesus was constantly praying to the Father, and the clarity that He had of the Father's purpose for His life was flawless. Jesus communicated with the Father like a bundled T-1 line, whereas our communication is often like a faulty dial-up. In cellphone terms, Jesus had four bars where we are often "searching for network." He was in constant communication with the Father because His Spirit and the Father's Spirit were one.

The physical input that Jesus received came through the same means as yours and mine. What He saw and heard with human eyes and ears while He was here on earth was no different than what you and I experience. The difference was His perfect communication with the Father directing Him in what to do through every step. He made this claim Himself: "I do nothing of My own, but speak just what the Father taught Me" (John 8:28). "[I] judge as God tells Me" (John 5:30). "[I see] what the Father is doing and go and do also" (John 5:19). "[I] do exactly what My Father commanded Me" (John 14:31).

It is this reliance on the Father—this dependence on the direction and guidance from the Holy Spirit—that we are to seek. When we operate from a pure heart, this communication channel becomes wide open. A pure heart is not a perfect heart; it's an honest one—a heart focused on truth. It's a heart that understands that we can trust God completely with our lives, and that we can actively "listen" for His input to direct our actions. Jesus stated that the pure in heart would "see God" (Matt.5:8). Jesus had a perfectly pure and sinless heart. Therefore, He clearly saw from the eternal perspective what the Father was doing. We can never match the heart of Jesus, but as we purify our hearts through our trust and surrender to Him, we too can gain a glimpse of that above-the-line view.

When we deviate from this process and rely on ourselves by having our "I"s fill our thoughts and take priority of our direction ("I will do this" or "I want that"), we clog our communication line with the Holy Spirit. The network traffic between the spirit and mind becomes busy or even disconnected, and we often miss the Holy Spirit's input.

Maintaining our communication with the Spirit is a difficult "skill," for lack of a better word, for many of us to develop. First, we are bombarded in this world through our sensory input. The vast majority of all marketing and advertising is designed to appeal to our "flesh" or physical nature. Every advertising firm knows that "sex sells." Unrestrained desire leads to coveting. The devil knows this, too. It's all very persuasive to our carnal needs. The "worries of this world" appear to scream at us for attention. It's hard to maintain a perspective from above the line when we're so immersed in the input from below the line. That's why prayer is so important. If we do not have that continuous attitude of prayer and frontal lobe focus on God's presence, then we are easily distracted.

Second, if we have an impulsive personality or have a take-charge attitude, then we have a tendency to "grab the ball and run with it," led by our own wisdom and intellect. We fail to pause to get that invaluable input from the Spirit. Though our intentions are good, we often "outrun our coverage."

It's a process. Like "total quality management" in the business world of continuous process improvement, the sanctification process in the spirit realm is the continuous pursuit of perfection—the pursuit of becoming Christ-like. It's a lifelong process. Don't overly worry about making mistakes. The apostle Paul assures us in his letter to the Romans that "we know that God causes all things to work together for good to those who love God, to those who are called according to His purpose" (Rom. 8:28 ESV).

The Father looks after His children, and He knows our hearts. If we seek His will through continual prayer and communication with His Spirit within us, then He will guide our steps. Make Jesus the Lord of your rings—the physical, mental/emotional, and spiritual aspects of you—and the Lord of your life. You will then walk in truth with a Kingdom-of-God perspective, and this view from above is an absolutely spectacular sight.

26. All In

Tom McAllister

America loves a winner. This is true in all circumstances, but especially true in sports. There is a thrill in the competition itself, and fan approval occurs when both competing parties give it their all.

Coaches employ a variety of motivational techniques to get the maximum effort from their players. Catchphrases are common:

"Finish the drill!"

"Give a hundred-and-ten percent."

"Go to the bell (or whistle)."

"Hold nothing back!"

"Gut check time!"

"Leave it on the field!"

In football, almost every team holds up four fingers to denote the fourth and final quarter and claim both their ownership of the end game and their commitment to give all they've got.

It's impressive to see the level of commitment and valiant effort by the players. Even fans cheer with great enthusiasm. Doesn't it seem logical or rational that we should have the same level of commitment and enthusiasm to our faith and spiritual walk in life? Shouldn't our commitment to the Creator of the universe be a little more important than a ball game? Shouldn't our zeal for the Lord, Who gave us the ability to compete, to perform, or even just to cheer, be the greatest motivation? Without Him, everything else goes away.

It's not like these are competing or mutually exclusive events. You can serve the Lord through your commitment to excellence in sports or whatever you do. As Paul wrote to the Colossians, "Whatever you do, work at it wholeheartedly as though you were doing it for the Lord and not merely for people" (Col. 3:23 ISV).

Strangely, it doesn't seem to work this way. The investment or level of commitment toward the Lord rarely surpasses the level of commitment to worldly things. Somehow, God gets left out or is given a back seat. If you ask someone if they believe in God, most will say yes. If you then ask how that belief affects their behavior in everyday life, then you get a few puzzled looks and a very diverse range of answers.

Aside from those who never acknowledge God at all, there appears to be three distinct strategies of an individual's commitment to their faith and spiritual walk. The first strategy is the Russian roulette method. This approach delays any sort of commitment to the Lord until the very last moment. The goal is to live your life your own way with you in control for as long as possible, with a planned conversion experience just before death. Their hero would be the one thief on the cross who asked Jesus to remember him when Jesus entered His Kingdom. He was assured a place in paradise just hours before his death. He did it his way until there were no more options—okay, he made it into Heaven, but notice that "his way" got him nailed to a cross in the first place.

Besides missing out on all the blessings in this lifetime of being in fellowship with our Lord, the danger of this approach is that you might "kick the bucket" before conversion. Now you're cooking not with fire, but in fire. Refer to the parable of the rich fool in Luke 12:16–21, for he thought he had it made and found out he had made the biggest mistake of all.

The second approach is the Hokie Pokie. Just like the song—put your left foot in, take your left foot out, put your left foot in, and shake it

130

all about—it's the I'm sorta committed thing. You know the type. They range from those who show up to church on Christmas and Easter to renew their "fire insurance" to those who treat church and faith as a task to complete—a section of their pie chart of time rather than a way of life in a spiritual relationship that permeates everything they do. They thank God when things luckily go their way and pray fervently when they are in need or trouble. The rest of the relationship is managed laissez faire or as needed basis.

These are lukewarm Christians, and Jesus doesn't have great things to say about that way of life. Refer to John's address to the church in Laodicea in Revelation 3:14–19 where Jesus says to those who are neither hot nor cold that He will spit them out of His mouth. Not a pretty picture is it?

The last group of people is like the gamblers in the Texas Hold'em World Series of Poker where they bet all their chips and go "all in." They push all their chips out on the table on one hand. In the spiritual analogy they would also dive on top of their chips on the table and commit their entire being. It's betting all you got—what you have materially, and your heart included.

This is the attitude of heart that pleases the Lord. He is the Great Coach, and He wants us to go all out, finish the drill, and leave it on the field. The other strategies at best yield little fruit and are dangerous tactics to employ. Why do something halfway? A half-hearted commitment toward anything demonstrates a genuine lack of faith.

Jesus taught many parables about the Kingdom of Heaven, or as He sometimes phrased it, the Kingdom of God. The Kingdom of Heaven is not just about Heaven. It's also about a way of living life to its fullest here on earth. It is a perspective of what is important and the first priority of what we are to pursue in life. It also guarantees that all our needs will be met. "But seek first His kingdom and His righteousness, and all these things will be added [provided] to you" (Matt. 6:33 NASB).

In chapter 13 of the book of Matthew, Jesus gave two of these parables: "The Kingdom of Heaven is like treasure hidden in a field. When a man found it, he hid it again, and then in his joy went and sold all he had and bought that field. Again, the Kingdom of Heaven is like a merchant looking for fine pearls. When he found one of great value, he went away and sold everything he had and bought it" (Matt. 13:44–46 NASB).

Notice that the approach of the main characters in these two parables is completely different. The first person was not looking for any treasure, but he discovered it. The second one was a seeker. He knew that something existed "out there" that had tremendous value. They came from totally opposite directions, the first uninformed, the second informed, but they both reached the same conclusion and made the same response. When they discovered the treasure (the Kingdom of Heaven), they sold all that they had in order to obtain it. They went "all in."

Is it worth the price? You bet your life. But don't feel bad about wondering as the disciple Peter implied his concern when he reminded Jesus, "We have left everything to follow you" (Mark 10:28 NIV). Jesus assured Peter that no one who left what they had for Him and the Gospel would fail to receive many times (100-fold) in this age and in the age to come, eternal life (Mark 10:29–30, Luke 18:29–30).

In this age of uncertain investing, there is one absolutely sure bet. Go all in—give all you have to Jesus, and you will reap an incredible return.

27. God's Own Agenda

Zoraya Valdez

While going on a missionary trip to Taiwan in the summer of 2009, I did not know what was in store for me, except that I was going to participate in the Vacation Bible School as teacher and in spreading the Gospel. My prayer was that the Lord would allow me to be one of His envoys. Even though we did not speak Mandarin or Cantonese, we communicated through interpreters with the people as they heard of Jesus and His love.

After traveling for almost twenty hours by plane and train to get to Taitug, we were happy and thankful that the Lord let us arrive in good spirits. Most importantly, I was thrilled to hear my dearest son Eliseo's voice by phone, as were the rest of my companions to hear their families when they called.

Every morning we would get up to have our group devotional and to plan our day. From there, we would go to a school to teach the Scriptures to the children of the area, as well as arts and crafts and fun games. We would spend a wonderful time with them regardless of the high humidity and the overwhelming heat that summer. At the end of our activities, we would return to plan visitation and spreading of the Gospel in the afternoons.

One particular afternoon, I was supposed to visit one of my students but instead I was assigned an unknown young man and his family. The only information I received was that he was seventeen years old and that he had a friend singing in the praise team at the local church. I meditated over this because I just did not know what to say. It was very natural to reach out to the children who attended my Bible class through games and teachings, but this new assignment felt very awkward to me. Nonetheless, I praised God for the opportunity to be chosen for that afternoon visit. As I went to the house with one of the interpreters, I asked God to give me the right words. I also wanted to be able to minister to the family according to their needs.

We walked for approximately three-quarters of a mile. When we arrived, a very kind family welcomed us with a delicious pineapple drink. I introduced myself as Zory, and I said that I was from Mexico. They were amazed that I had come from so far away and took the time to meet them. I thanked them for the privilege of letting me share the Good News with them. I asked if any of them had ever heard of Jesus. They responded that they had never heard of Him. I said that I wanted to tell them about the story of Jesus Christ.

The lady of the house, a mother of seven boys, told me that she did not believe that God would be willing to forgive her after having abandoned her family. She had just returned to them two months prior, but there was lots of friction and resentment among them. Tobi, the second child, asked me if God loved him, and why had He permitted his mother to abandon the children to the care of the grandmother, as this had caused the children great sorrow. Such was the opening I needed to speak about forgiveness. I directed my attention to the mother and asked for the reason behind her decision to leave the family. She said that her husband abused her daily, and that he treated the family dog nicer than he treated her. She said that she had left because she felt very desperate and humiliated. I felt compassion for her. You could tell she was struggling with her situation. She was very petite and somewhat frail, being not even 5 feet tall.

When she and I finished talking, I spoke to Tobi about his mother's suffering and despair I told him that I could feel how torn her heart was after being unable to forgive herself. I told Tobi and his mother that God offers forgiveness through Jesus, and that He already paid the debt of sin. When we confess Him as our Savior, He forgives us and cleanses us. As mentioned in Isaiah, God throws our sins to the ocean and never remembers them. I told them about Christ's love, salvation, and the redeeming grace of our Lord, and that He has given us the choice of forgiveness or bitterness in our hearts. We select to live miserably and to make others' lives miserable, or we select to forgive those who affect us emotionally and psychologically. God is the only Supreme Being Who has the power to restore a suffering person when he receives Jesus as his personal Savior. I told Tobi that not only does God forgive us, but He gives us the capacity to forgive. We cannot give what we do not have. At that precise moment, the mother said that she wanted to accept Jesus to be forgiven, so we prayed together, and then with the rest of the family. It was a moving experience. Unfortunately, we then had to say our goodbyes.

When we left, the interpreter told me that she had been blessed as well with the family. We started walking down the street, back to the church where my companions were waiting for us, when suddenly I heard somebody calling "Zory! Zory!" This is how I had introduced myself to the family because it was easier than trying to pronounce my name. So, it sounded very strange that someone was calling me by my nickname in such a remote place of the earth. Again I heard "Zoryyyyy." I turned to find out who was calling me, and I saw Tobi signaling for me to wait. When he finally reached us, breathless, and panting, he could only say: "I do not know when I will see you again, maybe never, but I need your Jesus. Please give me more of Jesus." In tears, he asked me not to leave before giving him more of Jesus, and for His forgiveness for himself and to be able to forgive his mom. He did not want a bitter heart. So we hugged and cried together in the middle of the street, and that is where he was saved. We prayed, and he thanked me for giving him the Good News. How wonderful to witness the miracle of forgiveness in the hearts of that family.

It was such a happy time. At that moment, I understood that although I wanted to visit one of my students, God had a perfect plan for that family. God had a different plan than mine, because He has His own agenda. We just need to be receptive. When it was time for me to be by myself, I started praying, thanking Him for letting me be a part of such an experience, and now for allowing me to share it with you.

28. Grape Expectations

Tom McAllister

In warfare, a key component to a successful attack strategy is to quickly disrupt your enemy's command and control. Disabling or hindering their internal communication significantly reduces their effectiveness to fight in a coordinated and cohesive manner. Units will be separated or cut off from others, their command centers will not have a grasp of the "big picture," and they will lack the necessary or vital information on how to best defend themselves. Uncertainty and isolation also adversely impacts their morale, which further decreases their effectiveness in battle.

In general, avoiding isolation and maintaining good communication is a key component to successful living. In today's information age, networking is an integral part of both business and society. There are many professional Web tools such as LinkedIn that enable you to maintain business contacts, find jobs or sales opportunities, and of course there are Facebook, MySpace, and Twitter to keep you in touch with your friends.

In the spiritual realm, staying connected is absolutely crucial.

Our Lord and Savior gave us a great analogy of this, as quoted by the Apostle John in his gospel:

I am the true vine, and My Father is the gardener. He cuts off every branch in Me that bears no fruit, while every branch that does bear fruit He prunes so that it will be even more fruitful. You are already clean because of the word I have spoken to you. Remain in Me, and I will remain in you. No branch can bear fruit by itself; it must remain in the vine. Neither can you bear fruit unless you remain in Me. I am the vine; you are the branches. If a man remains in Me and I in him, he will bear much fruit; apart from Me you can do nothing. If anyone does not remain in Me, he is like a branch that is thrown away and withers; such branches are picked up, thrown into the fire and burned. If you remain in Me and My words remain in you, ask whatever you wish, and it will be given you. This is to My Father's glory, that you bear much fruit, showing yourselves to be my disciples. As the Father has loved Me, so have I loved you. Now remain in my love. (John 15: 1–9, NIV).

Jesus is the vine and we are the branches. He is the Source of all that we have—the ability to live life abundantly and to produce fruit for His Kingdom. We can only do this if we are connected to Him. For a branch removed from the vine can do nothing on its own, and it will eventually wither and die. To put it more bluntly, if you (a branch) are separated from Jesus (the true Vine) and planted into the ground, then you're just a stick in the mud.

The Father is the gardener Who lovingly and tenderly takes care of the branches to enable them to be more fruitful. He lifts them up to get more sunlight ("Sonlight") and prunes and trims away the "wild shoots" so that the branches may grow more perfectly. As the psalmist stated in Psalm 33:13–15 (NIV/NLT): "The LORD looks from Heaven; He sees all mankind. From His throne He observes all who live on the earth. He made their hearts, so He understands everything they do."

The Father knows how to dress a vine so that it becomes more productive. He knows our hearts. As we grow and become bigger and stronger, what happens to us? We begin to look more and more like the vine itself. We become Christ-like.

Jesus is the "true" vine, implying that there are others that are false. The Father is the gardener Who oversees the entire vineyard (universe). Where's the third person of the Holy Trinity? He's the Life Force flowing through us. The Holy Spirit is the sap[1].

Okay, so it's a good analogy, but what's the practical application for all of this? Jesus tells us to remain or abide in Him. How do we do that? We do that through worship, fellowship with other believers, prayer, and reading of God's Word. Jesus is the Word—"And the Word became flesh and dwelt among us" (John 1:14). When we read God's Word, we open up ourselves for the sap, the Holy Spirit, to flow through us and give us wisdom, inspiration, and enlightenment. As you read the Scriptures, you will have more of those "aha" moments—similar to the situation the alcoholic describes as "a moment of clarity." These insights enable you to see God's plan for you more clearly, get the proper perspective on things, and discover the correct principles to embrace.

The second part of this connection is through prayer. We should pray unceasingly in all things. Prayer is where we open up our hearts to the Father, we give Him thanks, we state our needs, and we seek His guidance. When we are spiritually reborn, we are babies in the spirit, and that has nothing to do with our physical age. You can be very old physically and yet be a spiritual infant. Like an infant we initially have lots of needs and they take priority in our lives. We focus primarily on our needs and go to God as our Cosmic Genie with our wish list. We wonder if we pray correctly and if God is even hearing us. Don't get too wrapped up in the methodology. The Apostle Paul assures us that the Holy Spirit intercedes in our prayers:

> In the same way the Spirit also helps our weakness; for
> we do not know how to pray as we should, but the Spirit

Himself intercedes for us with groanings too deep for words; and He Who searches the hearts knows what the mind of the Spirit is, because He intercedes for the saints according to the will of God (Rom. 8:26–27 NASB).

Don't get frustrated. Be patient. As you grow in faith, you will grow in trust and you will gain more confidence in your communication efforts and prayer life. You will migrate from the infantile "God, what will you do for me?" to the mature "God, what will you do through me?"

The last pragmatic piece is the fellowship with other believers. Hang out with your fellow branches on the vine. Get involved with your church, your Sunday school, and the various missions and ministries that they have to offer. Therefore encourage one another and build each other up (1 Thess. 5:11). Compliment their "grapes", cheer on their growth, and be encouraged by them as well. We should be like the start of the church as told in Acts 2:42 NASB: "They devoted themselves to the apostles' teaching and to the fellowship, to the breaking of bread and to prayer." Grow your network of fellow Christians; there is strength and support in numbers.

Finally, what is the fruit that we are to produce? What will abiding in the vine of Christ, tended by the Father with the sap of the Holy Spirit cruising through us, accomplish? Paul tells us in Galatians 5:22–23 NLT: "But the Holy Spirit produces this kind of fruit in our lives: love, joy, peace, patience, kindness, goodness, faithfulness, gentleness and self-control."

Don't we all want those things in our lives? To be filled with love and joy and to have patience and peace no matter what our circumstances? Wouldn't it be enjoyable to share kindness, gentleness, and goodness with others and to do it out of faithful self-control? It's an awesome way to live. When you remain in Christ, you'll produce these fruits. You may ask whatever you wish and it will be given to you. Now, that sounds like a blank check from God. However, it's not necessarily anything you want, but anything you want *in accordance with the fruits of the Spirit of abiding in Christ.* If you have desires of the flesh or your sinful nature, then they will show up as: "sexual immorality, impurity and debauchery; idolatry and witchcraft; hatred, discord, jealousy, fits of rage, selfish ambition, dissensions, factions, and envy; drunkenness, orgies, and the like" (Gal. 5:19-21a). If this is your desire, then you are not a part of the true vine, and as Paul warns, "Those who live like this will not inherit the kingdom of God." (Gal. 5:21b).

Who wants to be filled with jealousy, rage, selfishness, and envy? What a stressful way to go through life. Don't let the devil disrupt your command and control and separate you from the love and spiritual nourishment of the Lord. Instead, choose a life abiding in Christ. It's the di**vine** way to live.

29. God Is in This!

Marcia Daniels

On January 12, 2010, the world stood still as Haiti experienced the most devastating earthquake known in its history. We said our prayers, gathered our composure, and continued our lives as Haitians began to dig through the rubble to find their loved ones and salvage what they could of their clothes and homes. Then the moral conscience kicked in and we began to assess the damage to determine what could be done to help thousands of mothers, fathers, families, and most of all orphaned children—children who were already orphans and those who became orphans as a result of losing their families.

Our church youth group at Bethlehem Star Baptist Church, Oklahoma City, Oklahoma, was already involved in sponsoring a child, Dachimeleck Dormainvil (Dach), through Compassion International. February 22, 2010, was Dach's birthday, and we still had no news of his whereabouts. We chose not to wait in silence but to reach out to all the children with what we called the Children–to–Children Haiti Project.

Our children decorated empty containers that previously held nutritional powder (better known as nutritional shakes) for the children in Port-au-Prince, Haiti. The cans were a perfect size for holding various sundries. We then gathered soap, washcloths, toothpaste and brushes, candy, toy cars for the boys, and chapstick for the girls. Each gift was designed to let them know how special they are to Jesus and to us. When it came time to ship the containers, we realized there was no place in Haiti where they could be delivered, as we had no shipping address or point of contact.

Although God had already spoken to me and told me to tell Reliv, the manufacturer of those nutritional shakes, what we were doing with their cans, I did not. Instead, I listened to others' doubts and fears of sharing this information for fear it would not be received well.

Push came to shove as it often does, and I finally turned to Reliv International. I told them what we were doing with these super-sturdy Reliv cans that were relatively clean after they were used. They were very excited!

This was a relief. And yet while the news pleased Reliv International, we were still lacking a way to ship the cans to Haiti. I told Reliv about the problem. It was a Wednesday afternoon, and Reggie Ament from Reliv's Kalogris Foundation said, with excitement, "Marcia, this is God's timing."

Imagine that.

She said: "We are on our way to Port-au-Prince a week from Friday. If you can get them shipped to Kathy Brawley and Maybeeline Dungue-Despagne by Monday, we'll take them with us." I was so shocked and excited all at the same time, I could hardly contain myself.

This company had no reason to help me or our church youth with our mission project. I had already contacted several relief organizations, and they would only accept financial donations, or packages shipped a certain way.

I was very relieved that I did not have to return to our youth to tell them that we could not ship their gifts to Haiti. For more than twenty-two years, Reliv's mission has been to "Nourish the World," in mind, body, and spirit. For those who dared to believe, we learned that this is truly a company with a heart. Their mission has transcended into their everyday life so much that it is the norm.

The story only gets better from here. While our church was very capable and willing to pay the shipping, I knew that we would not be able to contact our finance department prior to the shipping date, so I called Reggie and explained our dilemma.

She said, "Marcia, just tell me how many boxes you have, and where and what time we can pick them up." Who would not want to partner with a company like this?

After all the packages were ready to be shipped, I put a bright pink heart on all the boxes because the gifts were made, shipped, and delivered with love. Reliv International agreed to ship our cans, pay the shipping, pick them up at the designated shipping location, and carry them into Port-au-Prince.

Wow. I knew God was involved, but I was still amazed when the project came full circle beyond my expectations. Reliv continued to use their resources to send our children pictures and video clips of the children receiving their individually packaged cans of goodies from children in the United States. Now our children who otherwise would not have experienced the faces and smiles of the Haitian children were able to see the rewards of their labor. At this point, we still had not found Dach, but I knew that God was taking care of him.

Why did I second-guess the prompting of the Holy Spirit? I knew strongly in my spirit that I was to tell Reliv that we were recycling their cans in a Haiti project. Before I contacted all those other organizations, I knew I was supposed to contact Reliv, but I used my own human reasoning. When all else failed, I heard "I told you...," so I immediately called Reliv.

Reggie confirmed what I already knew, "Marcia, God is in this."

This is how God uses willing vessels to help His children. If we would just listen with our hearts and obediently follow the lead of the Holy Spirit, we can do amazing things for our world and for the Kingdom. I can only imagine how much more amazing this project could have been had I contacted Reliv first.

We must move in God's timing. God arranged for Reggie to be on her way to Port-au-Prince just in time to deliver our gifts to the Haitian children.

God is the same, yesterday, today, and forever (Hebrews 13:8). In the same way, He sent the prophet Elijah to the city of Zarephath (1 Kings 17:10) to provide for a widow and her son. However, God ordered Elijah's steps so that he arrived just in time. First, because of a severe drought in the land, He sent him eastward to the brook Cherith. There, God provided him with food, bread, and water from the brook to drink. However, after a time, God dried up the brook and He told Elijah to go to another city (v. 8). "Then the word of the Lord came to him saying, arise and go to Zarephath, which belongs to Sidon and stay there; behold I have commanded a widow to provide for you." This was God's way of providing for the widow whom He knew needed food. With God there are no coincidences. "The mind of a man plans his way, but the Lord directs his steps" (Proverbs 16:9 ESV).

When Elijah arrived, he found a widow gathering sticks for a fire so that she could prepare her last meal for her son and herself and then die (1 Kings 17: 12). Just in time, God told Elijah how to provide for her and her son. The Bible says, "She went and did according to the word of Elijah, and she and her family ate for many days" (1 Kings 17: 15).

If Elijah had argued with God, debated where God was telling him to go or what to do, the widow and her son would have died. When God is in it, He will direct the footsteps of the righteous and He will do it just in time. We have to be obedient and move as He directs us. No matter how odd things may appear, we must be obedient and move in His timing. I am so grateful that I finally called Reliv. A few days later, it would have been too late.

As for Reliv, a company does not become extraordinary on its own but it takes like-minded employees and leaders. So how did Reggie know that her organization would support this endeavor that she so eagerly embraced? It occurred to me that Reliv is the perfect example of all the old-school teachings, that leadership starts at the top and it trickles down throughout the organization. Apparently, Reliv's leaders, Robert and Sandy Montgomery, have been leading and modeling their mission, vision, and goals for the twenty-plus years that they have been in business. Reggie had already caught the vision and the mission and was running with it, delivering tents, shakes, and much more when we came along. We were another opportunity.

Some more good news: Dach, the child we were sponsoring, was later found to be safe and unharmed.

30. Who's Your Daddy? Part I

Tom McAllister

A common error made in the business world is the sense of urgency to start creating potential solutions to an issue before you've properly defined the problem. There's a sarcastic adage to this approach, "There's not enough time to do it right, but there's enough time to do it over." Trial and error, however, is typically an expensive methodology to employ.

The first step in problem solving is to accurately identify and define what the problem is. If you fail in this objective, then you end up solving symptoms of the problem that may not bring about a worthwhile solution and in many cases will make things worse. In the consulting world, one effective tool in troubleshooting a complex problem is Root Cause Analysis or 5Y as it sometimes called. It's a simple approach by asking a series of "Why" questions. Typically it takes no more than five "Whys," thus the name 5Y, to discover the root source of the problem.

Take for example the banking financial crisis that came to a head in late 2008. Why was there a financial crisis? Banks and financial/lending institutions were not adequately liquid to loan money to keep commerce flowing. Why were these institutions not sufficiently liquid? They had too many "toxic assets" on their balance sheets. Why did they have too many toxic assets on their balance sheets? They made too many loans to marginally or under qualified people who defaulted on their loans. Why did they make too many loans to under qualified people? The federal government relaxed lending standards and pressured these institutions to make these loans, and well, you get the picture. You keep digging until you find the root cause.

Now this is an oversimplified illustration for a complex issue, but the concept and process works just the same. Had a detailed analysis of the financial crisis been conducted, perhaps a more viable solution could have been developed than to just "throw money at it." This seems to be the standard knee-jerk reaction the federal government always makes. Unfortunately, the money we're now "throwing" at problems is not even our own. Our country is so broke that we have to borrow money from someone else to just be able to throw it. That's embarrassing.

So let's move away from inept political problem solving and tackle the most important question of all. This question has plagued mankind from the moment he had the ability to contemplate it. This is the Mother of all Root Causes. How did we get here and why are we here at all?

To tackle this problem, we'll begin by analyzing this grand universe in which we live. Let's take a look at what's going on out there and see if it has any clues. First, we'll start with a little background information.

Back in the 1920s, Edwin Hubble (the astronomer that the Hubble Telescope is named after) made some startling discoveries about the stars in the sky. This discovery blew our minds with our concept of the size of the universe. It was larger—*much larger*—than we thought. The prevailing thought at that time was that our galaxy, the Milky Way, was about the extent of our universe. Hubble began to see galaxies beyond our own galaxy, and not just one, but millions of them. Millions of galaxies containing billions of stars demonstrated a huge expanse of the universe in which we live. It's really quite big.

As Hubble began to study these distant galaxies, he received some puzzling results. The light frequencies or color that he expected to see did not correspond with what he observed. What he noticed was that there was a uniform shift in the color and appearance of distant objects. Objects appeared to be more red than forecasted. This gave rise to the term "red shift" or a shifting to red end of the spectrum of light. Here's the first "Why." *Why did these galaxies appear more red than expected?* To interpret this phenomenon, Hubble applied the concept of the Doppler Effect.[1]

Now you NASCAR fans are very familiar with the Doppler Effect. Vocally imitate the sound of Greg Biffle, Kyle Busch, Danica Patrick or your favorite driver's car as it goes by on the track. If there are other people in the room and they are now staring at you, do not worry. You're just following instructions. Imitate the sound again, even louder this time just to pique their curiosity. Notice how the pitch changes. As the car approaches, the pitch is higher and as it passes and moves away from you the pitch goes lower. This is the Doppler Effect. As an object comes toward you, it compresses the sound waves and causes them to scrunch up and be higher in frequency. As the object moves away from you, the sound waves elongate and the pitch gets lower. If you're a weather watcher fanatic, then you probably heard the weatherman talk about their Doppler radar, which tracks storms using the Doppler Effect to determine the direction the storms are heading.

Light behaves in a similar fashion. When light approaches you, it increases in frequency, and it decreases in frequency when it moves away. For visible light, higher frequencies exist in the blue and violet spectrum and the lowest frequency (longest wavelength) is red. When Hubble studied far away galaxies and noticed that the objects appeared redder than they should, this indicated that the objects were moving away. This meant that the universe was expanding. Here's the second "Why." *Why was the universe expanding?* Thinking backwards in time, if the universe was expanding, then the stars were closer to us last week, last month, last year, and so on. If you continue this reverse time engineering long enough, you will reach a point in time where the entire universe is simply that—a point. A point of singularity where the entire universe is compressed into something that has virtually no size. We're talking way smaller than the period at the end of this sentence. That's pretty astounding.

To go back any further we end up with nothing. Now here's the final "Why." *Why did the universe go from nothing to something?* The answer to this folks is the Mother of all Root Causes.

We really have just two choices. The first is that we have a Creator Who pressed the cosmic start button that caused the universe to exist. The second possibility is that it just happened. Let's consider the latter solution for a moment, "It happened." This reminds me of a vulgar bumper sticker that was popular in the 1980s. It rhymes with "it happens," but I'll paraphrase here: *Poop Happens.*

There you go—the Mother of all Root Causes, the apex of scientific achievement and knowledge, the primal cause of our existence is that Poop Happens. Makes you feel good about the intellectual advancement of our species doesn't it? I wonder if the guy who coined the phrase (I'm assuming it's a guy as ladies typically don't use such language although some do when severely agitated) realized that he was formulating the ultimate theoretical answer to the ultimate human question (*Why are we here?*) and establishing the cornerstone of the philosophical and religious belief of the atheist. It's amazing what a simple bumper sticker can do. Yet several people (we will hence refer to them as Poopy Heads) subscribe to this theory. They have added complexity and various twists to the baseline Poop Theory—the Big Bang/Big Crunch theory, wherein the universe is an eternal accordion of expansion and then contraction and then expansion again, or the colliding membrane theory where multiple universes collide, or the multiple universe theory itself, but when stripped of all the extraneous postulating and tested with mathematical models, they are simply just full of poop. To dispel this theory even further, you can't even have poop without a pooper.

There is only one answer to this ultimate question: *God did it*.

It is not only the most logical answer, but it's the only answer with any logic. If you cannot see this truth, then your vision may be obscured because you have your hips on your shoulders (you may be a Poopy Head).

The pursuit of knowledge and truth has taken mankind on an incredible journey. Through the amazing achievements of science we have validated with mathematical theory and proof the origin of our universe and confirmed what theologians have known for thousands of years. The answer is contained in the leadoff sentence of His handbook inspirationally written for us: "In the beginning, God created the Heavens and the earth" (Gen. 1:1 ESV).

31. Who's Your Daddy? Part II

Tom McAllister

Science has made incredible discoveries over the past hundred years. In the last century, great strides were made both in the smallest realm of our existence, quantum physics, to the grand "big picture" of our universe through astronomy.

The scientific quest continues. In the atomic particle accelerator experiments conducted in the international CERN research center, a huge tunnel between France and Switzerland, scientists try to smash particles together to simulate the conditions of the universe when it was very young—fractions of a second old. New particles are being discovered and old ones like protons and neutrons have been broken down into smaller entities such as up quarks and down quarks. The electrons are still around, but we also have bosons, muons, tauons, and gluons. Who is coming up with these names? It seems like the physics department must be downwind of the chemistry lab and is inhaling too many hallucinogenic vapors.

In astronomy, technological advancements in telescope design have enabled scientists to see galaxies at the very perimeter of our universe billions of light-years away. The expanse of this universe is incredible and awe-inspiring.

When you use a scientific eye to view how the universe was made and how it operates, you discover some statistics that are simply amazing. Below are just a few:

- Protons are 1,836 times the size of electrons. If this ratio was just a little larger or smaller, then we would not exist due to the inability of the correct molecules to form that we require for life. Likewise, if their respective charges were not exactly opposite (protons +1 and electrons -1), then we would not exist.

- Water is one of the rare molecules that expands and is less dense in solid form than it is in liquid form. This allows ice to float. Without this property, ice would sink, the earth would become a frozen ball, and life could not exist.

- Our position in our solar system and in our Milky Way galaxy is within extremely fine tolerances of the amount of heat, cold, and cosmic radiation to support life.

- If our day (rate of rotation of the earth) was either shorter or longer, if the moon was closer or further away, or if the earth's axis was tilted greater or less, then life could not exist on this planet.

- If the force of gravity was too weak, then stars would never have initiated nuclear fusion and thus create light. If too strong, stars would burn too quickly and be too erratic to support life.

- The force that holds particles together within the nucleus of an atom is called the strong nuclear force. If this force was too weak, then only hydrogen and helium would have been formed and the universe would be just space. If too strong, then mostly heavy elements would have formed and there would be not enough light elements to create life.

✳ The electromagnetic force is the force that bonds electrons to the nucleus. If too weak, electrons would not stay in orbit. If too strong, then electrons would not bond with other atoms. In either case, there would be no molecules.

If you were walking along a beach and you kicked up a cell phone buried in the sand, you wouldn't exclaim, "Wow, what a cool-looking rock or seashell." You would immediately recognize it as being manmade. When you look at our universe and at the life living in it, you should instantly recognize the evidence of design everywhere. Whether looking through a telescope, a microscope, or just using the naked eye, we should easily see "Made by God" stamped on everything we view. This universe is not some cosmic accident. It is not the result of an unfathomable and mathematically impossible series of random and chance events that produced life here on earth. This universe is so incredibly fine-tuned and designed to accuracies so far beyond our human capability that we all should simply stare in slack-jawed awe and marvel. When you contemplate all the intricacies involved, it is readily apparent that our universe is precisely designed to support the life that we know and experience. Paul stated this obvious observation in his letter to the Romans: "They know the truth about God because He has made it obvious to them. For ever since the world was created, people have seen the earth and sky. Through everything God made, they can clearly see His invisible qualities—His eternal power and divine nature" (Rom. 1:19–20a NLT).

Now here's the catchphrase, and it's quite condemning: "So they have no excuse for not knowing God." (Rom. 1:20b NLT)

No excuse.

Why is it that there are so many people oblivious to the obvious? There are perhaps many reasons, but upon deeper analysis you'll eventually uncover the root cause—pride. Pride is a blinder to the truth and a distorter of the truth, for it disrupts the proper perspective and priority of the universe. Pride is like cataracts on your spiritual eyes. Whether it's one's pride in one's own intellect, pride in self-determining will, or pride in the ability of science or other manmade endeavors, the priority is always wrong if it does not place God first. The worst scenario is not acknowledging God at all. Any person who follows this path is walking in utter darkness.

Now here's the good news: Jesus is the Light of the world. He will bring those who follow Him out of their darkness and "to all who believe in Him and accept Him, He gives the right to become children of God" (John 1:12). Having Jesus Christ as your Lord and receiving His Spirit gives you eternal life and makes you an heir in God's Kingdom.

Further on in Paul's letter to the Romans, he states, "For you did not receive a spirit that makes you a slave again to fear, but you received the Spirit of sonship. And by Him we cry, 'Abba, Father'" (Rom. 8:15 NIV). In Galatians, Paul states virtually the same thing in verse 4:6: "And because we are His children, God has sent the Spirit of his Son into our hearts, prompting us to call out, 'Abba, Father.'"

Abba is an endearing term children use for their Father. The best English translation is *Papa* or *Dad*. That's how intimate God, the Creator of this vast and amazing universe, wants His relationship to be with His children. He wants us to call Him Daddy. Imagine that. The Creator of the universe of which materially we are just a small and insignificant piece wants to be so involved in our lives and so joined in our relationship to Him that we address Him as Father—we address Him as Dad. That's beyond humbling. He wants us to take His hand and look forward to each new day with an expectant attitude of "What are we going to do today, Daddy?"

Like little children on the playground, we can brag about our Daddy—and we can do so with absolute honesty. Our Daddy can whip anyone else's daddy, and He is the greatest Dad there is.

32. Price Is Right

Tom McAllister

Many of you may recall the movie starring Robert Redford, Demi Moore, and Woody Harrelson entitled *Indecent Proposal*. In it, Moore and Harrelson play a recently married couple, and Redford is a wealthy businessman who offers the couple a million dollars to spend one night with Harrelson's wife, Demi Moore. This was yet another Hollywood saga addressing the age-old question, *"Does everything have a price?"*

Often the price tag is not stated in such a stark, vulgar fashion. However, in every decision you make, there is a mental calculation of the return on investment (ROI). Is the anticipated goal, objective, or reward worth the cost to obtain it? This gets trickier when aspects of character, such as honor or integrity, are pitted against worldly values, such as money or fame. Sometimes there is no reward. It is simply a matter of minimizing costs, and most of us are very adverse to risk. Standing up for what is right is rarely easy.

So, what's the price? What cost would you incur to maintain your integrity? Do you avoid the shade in your business dealings, or is there an illegal gap in your GAAP (Generally Accepted Accounting Principles)? Are you faithful in your marriage? Do you bend the rules like a Gumby doll when doing your taxes? How firm would you stand to protect your good name and adhere to your principles? Would you bet your life?

About two thousand six hundred years ago, such a moral dilemma occurred, and to government officials no less. Their story is recorded in the third chapter of the book of Daniel. Many of you are familiar with it. It's a story of three young men who faced a simple choice with immense consequences: Shadrach, Meshach, and Abednego. The king they faced was the great king of Babylon, Nebuchadnezzar.

King Nebuchadnezzar had conquered Judea and taken the people captive. As a practice, he took many of his best and brightest captives, submitted them to reeducation programs, and then brought them into his court. Shadrach, Meshach, and Abednego were three Hebrews taken into captivity and retrained for the king's service. They performed well, and as a result, they were promoted as officials and administrators over the province of Babylon itself.

The king decided to erect a ninety-foot golden statue befitting his ego, and he created a rule that when certain music played, everyone had to bow down and worship the golden image. If anyone did not bow down, he or she would be thrown into a furnace of blazing fire.

The music was played and the people all worshipped—except for Shadrach, Meshach, and Abednego. They were brought before Nebuchadnezzar. The king, though enraged, must have liked these three, for he gave them another opportunity to comply just in case they "didn't get the memo." He said to them, "I will give you one more chance to bow down and worship the statue I have made when you hear the sound of the musical instruments. But if you refuse, you will be thrown immediately into the blazing furnace. And then what god will be able to rescue you from my power?" (Dan. 3:15 NLT).

Cut!

Now, let's bring you in as a Hebrew stunt double. Here's the scene: You're an influential administrator over the capital city of the most powerful empire of the world. It's a great job, the pay is generous, the food and amenities are excellent, and you get to hang out and rule with a couple of good buddies. Life is more than just good—it's really good.

True, you have a highly arrogant, egotistical king as a boss, and he's a bit spun up at the moment, and when he's mad, the vein on his forehead sticks out like a Klingon warrior's. He wants to show everyone who's boss, and all you have to do is quickly bow down to his goofy golden statue, and then you're done with it, and everyone can move on, and it's back to the good life. Otherwise, it's over, rover; you're furnace-bound to become administrator *au flambeau.*

Now—*action!*

What would you do? Would you *bow* to the pressure?

Since most of us would blow our lines under such a fiery scenario, let's go back and take a seat. We'll reinsert the original cast and learn from the professionals. Here's how Shadrach, Meshach, and Abednego responded:

> "O Nebuchadnezzar, we do not need to defend ourselves before you. If we are thrown into the blazing furnace, the God whom we serve is able to save us. He will rescue us from your power, Your Majesty. But even if He doesn't, we want to make it clear to you, Your Majesty, that we will never serve your gods or worship the gold statue you have set up" (Dan. 3:16–18 NLT).

How's that for a response to a literal trial by fire?

It certainly didn't appease the king, as that Klingon vein glazed purple and doubled in size. He ordered the temperature of the furnace to be turned up seven times hotter than usual, and he had his guards tie up the hands and feet of the three Hebrews. When the guards opened the furnace door, the flames leaped out and killed them, and Shadrach, Meshach, and Abednego, still tied up, fell into the furnace. Then King Nebuchadnezzar leapt to his feet in amazement and asked his advisers, "Weren't there three men that we tied up and threw into the fire?" They replied, "Certainly, O king." He answered and said, "But I see four men unbound, walking in the midst of the fire, and they are not hurt; and the appearance of the fourth is like a son of the gods" (Dan. 3:24–25 NLT).

> Nebuchadnezzar then approached the opening of the blazing furnace and shouted, "Shadrach, Meshach, and Abednego, servants of the Most High God, come out. Come here." So Shadrach, Meshach and Abednego came out of the fire. Then the high officers, officials, governors, and advisers crowded around them and saw that the fire had not touched them. Not a hair on their heads was singed, and their clothing was not scorched. They didn't even smell of smoke. Then Nebuchadnezzar said, "Praise to the God of Shadrach, Meshach, and Abednego. He sent His angel to rescue His servants who trusted in Him. They defied the king's command and were willing to die rather than serve or worship any god except their own God" (Dan. 3:26–28 NIV).

Even an arrogant king can recognize the actions of the true God. Nebuchadnezzar then declared, "Therefore I decree that the people of any nation or language who say anything against the God of Shadrach, Meshach, and Abednego will be torn limb from limb, and their houses will be turned into heaps of rubble. There is no other god who can rescue like this" (Dan. 3:29 NIV).

Well, that turned out all right.

When you're with God, it always does. Wouldn't it be great if our leaders behaved with such integrity and devotion to the God we ask to bless this nation? Let's try to elect some leaders like this. When we say, "God bless America," our leaders and we citizens should mean it, and our attitude and behavior should fully align with our request. Let's cease and desist from this political correctness nonsense that has permeated our society. If we believe in God and follow His Son, then let's have the courage to speak it and to live it even if this causes our situation to get a little heated.

There is a consequence to every decision we make, and everything has a cost or a price. There are some things, however, that money cannot buy, and some things that money shouldn't buy, and there are some things that you should never sell.

There is a price to pay for being a follower of Christ. We all must pick up our cross and follow Him. We should always look past the cost and focus on the reward—the Return on Investment. God advertises His rewards program through His Word found in the Bible. It is the ultimate Truth in advertising, and His benefits package is so incredible that "No eye has seen, no ear has heard, and no mind has imagined what God has prepared for those who love Him" (1 Cor. 2:9 NLT).

So, speaking of Adonai advertising, we'll conclude with this compelling Christian commercial message:

Honoring the newborn King:	gold, frankincense, or myrrh
Price to convert a rogue disciple to a traitor:	thirty pieces of silver
Having the Son of God die for you as payment for all your sins:	priceless

There are some things that our money can buy; the most important thing however, has to be obtained through grace—amazing grace—how sweet the sound. It sounds like...love.

33. The Death of an Institution

Rick Saltzer

*t*he word was out, the finger had written,
  the box was open, the hand been bitten! –
studies completed, all findings were fair,
  data dissected, no margin for error! –
analysis pure, nothing refuted,
  the experts were sure, the case concluded! –

The Pillar collapsed, the Culture undone,
  Tradition erased and *Chaos* begun!:

  .... marches were canceled and protests recalled,
    everywhere writers were "shocked and appalled" –
  pundits were puzzled and poets were vexed,
    media muzzled and artists perplexed –
  news anchors sadly swallowed a sob,
    street preachers rudely thrown out of a job –
  academics took a shot to the crotch,
    professors were put on suicide watch –
  magazines folded and mayors resigned,
    bureaucracies completely realigned –
  movies and screenplays were forced to be trashed,

the thespian world was suddenly smashed –
colleges became financially strapped,
    large chunks of valued curricula scrapped –
musicians and singers ran out of steam,
    television shows were stripped of their theme –
journalists panicked with nothing to write –
    attorneys frantically searched for a fight –
political parties were equally stunned,
    nobody could tell which victims to fund. . . .

.... on that fateful day when Racism ended,
    it's safe to say confusion abounded –
the crutch on which so many depended
    gave way and left the country confounded –

a staple of everyday life removed,
    it was unclear how the people should act –
but with the new view, the nation improved,
    and the mayhem caused couldn't change that fact –

now with The Skin-Pigment Problem resolved,
    the national scene would change forever –
the Race-Based endeavors were all dissolved,
    and Colors allowed to blend together. . . .

34. No Pain No Gain

Tom McAllister

In metallurgy, there are several ways to increase the strength of steel. One is *strain hardening*, where the metal is beaten or bent, which causes the crystal structure of the atoms to become dislocated, and this makes the material stronger. Another is *tempering*, which exposes the steel to extremely hot temperatures. This also causes microstructure realignment within the steel to increase its strength. Heat and stress improve the strength and quality of steel.

In a sense, the same is true for us humans. I'm not speaking of locking people in a sauna and then beating them up. Physiologically, to increase muscle size and density, you strain and stress the muscles, which causes them to break down, restructure, and grow. This process takes time in the physical body, unlike steel, in which the process happens rapidly.

Getting into good physical shape is a goal for many, yet it is accomplished by few. It takes time and commitment to achieve. For our military members, physical fitness is extremely important, and each branch of service periodically tests its service men and women to ensure that certain standards are met. Back when I was in the service, most of the testing criteria were the same for all the services except for the run component. The few and the proud of the Marine Corps did a three-mile run while the Army, being all that they can be, did a two-mile run, and the Navy only ran for a mile and a half. I never understood why Navy personnel had to run that far. The longest warship is less than twelve hundred feet long, so there's only so far you can go. If we had sufficient faith to walk on water, then we might have to train to go hundreds of miles, but that's a completely different type of skill set.

As for the Air Force, they didn't even do a run. They had some type of stress test, which, based on an unconfirmed rumor, consisted of being able to set up a lounge chair by the pool and order drinks within, say, a five-minute period. I think the drinks had to have those fancy umbrellas in them as well. Having sufficient shade for the ice cubes so that they do not melt too fast is critical.

In a more serious light, if you want to grow and excel in a particular endeavor, you have to work at it. It takes hours of training and practice to hone your skills and talents. This is true in all aspects of life, and physical training may be the quickest to develop. Malcolm Gladwell, author of several best-selling books and selected in 2005 by *Time* magazine as one of the country's one hundred most influential people, refers to the concept of the ten-thousand-hour rule. He further states that when analyzing any kind of cognitively complex field such as diagnostic medicine, playing chess, or creative writing, it typically takes around ten thousand hours of practice before one is able to master it. That's roughly twenty hours per week for ten years. It takes the human brain that long to assimilate all the cognitive skills necessary to achieve true mastery.

The same path for skill growth is true for our spiritual walk in life. Once you accept Christ as your personal Savior, you do not instantly purge all of your bad habits and suddenly gain massive amounts of godly wisdom. You are a new person in the spiritual, but you still have the same body and brain cells. As the apostle Paul wrote to the new members in the church in Corinth (1 Cor. 3:2 NLT), "I had to feed you with milk, not with solid food, because you weren't ready for anything stronger. And you still aren't ready." It's a process that takes time no different than an exercise regime to improve your physical skills or a prolonged period of studying to increase your mental abilities.

Like cross training with weightlifting, aerobic exercise, and other physical drills, there are methods to employ to improve your spiritual knowledge, insight, and growth. Bible study, prayer, praise and worship, fasting, assembling with other believers, having an accountability partner, mentoring and discipleship programs, and many other tools enable you to grow in Christ. The ways in which you utilize these tools will improve your results.

In weight training, you can go into a gym and use various machines in an ad hoc fashion, and you will grow in strength. However, having a well-defined weight-lifting program will get you better results faster. Similarly, being disciplined in your approach to spiritual growth will enhance that growth. The caution is not to be too focused on the methodology itself. Remember, this is about a relationship between you and your Heavenly Father. Prayer and praise, Bible study, and fasting are simply methods to train your heart toward God. It's not as if God will bless you more if you pray with your hands folded in a certain way. It's developing the proper attitude of heart that matters most.

Along the way, there will be testing. College football athletes hoping to make it to professional football often go through a series of tests called the combine. They are tested in the forty-yard dash, the vertical leap, and various other drills. Those going into professions requiring certification often have to pass tests such as the CPA exam, the professional engineer exam, or the bar exam. [The latter is for those going into the legal profession, not a "name that beer" contest at the local pub]. When you start your training program to follow Christ, prepare to be tested. God will test the "mettle" of your faithfulness as preparation for greater responsibility in the promotion of His Kingdom. Do not be afraid of this. God will never test you more than you can handle. He is grooming you for an earthly promotion—increasing your wattage so that you can shine brighter for the Lord. The apostle Peter gives us a heads-up on this when he writes, "These trials will show that your faith is genuine. It is being tested as fire tests and purifies gold—though your faith is far more precious than mere gold. So when your faith remains strong through many trials, it will bring you much praise and glory and honor on the day when Jesus Christ is revealed to the whole world" (1 Pet. 1:7 NLT).

Later, in the fourth chapter of 1 Peter, the apostle encourages believers to be glad under such "fiery trials." He writes:

> Dear friends, don't be surprised at the fiery trials you are going through, as if something strange were happening to you. Instead, be very glad--for these trials make you partners with Christ in His suffering, so that you will have the wonderful joy of seeing His glory when it is revealed to the entire world" (1 Pet. 4:12–13 NLT).

The phrase "no pain, no gain" obviously applies to our spiritual walk. Going through the valley is never easy, but there is great reward on the other side. Our faith is broken down and restructured so that it is stronger. When we look into the rearview mirror, we're amazed at what we've been through, and we know Who got us through it. The fiery trial emblazons a great motto on our hearts: "I can do all things through Christ Who strengthens me" (Phil. 4:13 WEB).

These types of "God-permitted" trials, however, are not to be confused with the difficulties that result from our own errors. Our screw-ups are not part of God's plan. The hardships that follow them are simply the natural consequences of our own foolishness. Peter also addresses this type of circumstance and makes the distinction: "Of course, you get no credit for being patient if you are beaten for doing wrong. But if you suffer for doing good and endure it patiently, God is pleased with you" (1 Pet. 2:20 NLT).

In the Navy, the court system for handling minor offenses is called

Captain's Mast. Sailors can find all sorts of ways to misbehave, and when they do, they are required to appear before the commanding officer to receive judgment for their offenses. Often the punishment is extra duty or restriction to the ship or base, but in more severe cases, there can be heavy fines and/or a demotion to a lower pay grade. I once served under a commanding officer who often made this rather harsh but true observation to the sailors who appeared before him at Captain's Mast: "Life is tough. It's even tougher when you're stupid."

This is raw reality. We are all going to face difficult seasons of time and tests in our lifetime. We should do our best not to add to that burden. Stupidity is never beneficial. Minimizing the Homer Simpson *d'oh* moments in our lives should be a KPI (Key Performance Indicator). We should be wise in all that we do, for wisdom helps us to recognize pitfalls, and it enables us to avoid them. When we analyze our regrets in life, how often do they point back to an unwise decision made somewhere along the way? The statistics are pretty close to 100 percent accurate on that.

When we contemplate and do a "lessons learned" exercise to review our mishaps, we discover that most of our self-made catastrophes did not hinge on a single decision, but were a full string of less-than-wise decisions that led to the tragic outcome. Most addicts did not start out with the intention of becoming addicted. Very few people stand at the altar exchanging marriage vows while plotting their first extramarital affair. Yet addiction and affairs happen all the time, and the ensuing train wrecks leave emotional pain and carnage everywhere in their wake. If we are not diligent in our spiritual focus, or if we get lazy in our spiritual training, we can pull a Humpty Dumpty and have a great fall. That one "aw, shucks" can wipe out a lifetime of "attaboys." Sometimes our shortsighted actions can have long-term negative consequences. It's never what it's cracked up to be—ask ol' HD; he was never put back together again.

The apostle Paul warns us of this. In his letter to the Ephesians, he advises, "So then, be very careful how you live. Don't live like foolish people, but like wise people. Make the most of your opportunities because these are evil days" (Eph. 5:15–16 GWT).

It is a bad, bad world out there. How many scams exist on just the Internet of thieves wanting to steal our identities or defraud us of money? I never knew I had so many wealthy relatives in Nigeria wanting to send me incredible sums of money if I just give them my bank account number. We can even screw up closer to home with our friends. How often have you followed along with your friends just to have fun, and it led to disaster? There was no malice involved—but there was no wisdom, either.

Preventive maintenance is always much cheaper than corrective maintenance, or as the saying goes, "An ounce of prevention equals a pound of cure." We should incorporate wisdom and ethical principles into our daily lives to serve as a warning to us and sound the alarm, "Warning! Warning! Danger, Will Robinson!" before we get *Lost in Space* or do something foolish. We need to put up behavioral guardrails that are not placed as a last stand at the edge of the abyss, but are sufficiently far enough away to prevent disaster. Instead of thinking you can handle recreational drug use, don't even start down that path, as it could lead to addiction. Be careful and set boundaries around how you behave in social settings with co-workers so that you don't get into an emotional affair, or worse, a physical one that destroys a marriage. Be alert and be prepared. "Those who are prudent see danger and take refuge, but the naïve continue on and suffer the consequences" (Prov. 27:12 ISV). Try to identify your trouble areas and steer clear of them. It will save you many headaches in the future.

As part of the initial indoctrination process for future consultant employees in my former consulting firm, we asked them to describe the skills and character traits found in a good consultant. Though we often got a diverse set of answers, most recognized the value of a strong work ethic, honesty, and successfully meeting the customers' needs. Consultants always speak of "best practices" or the right way to solve a particular problem or manage a specific project. The term "best practices" encompasses the business-consulting idea of wisdom. Our company even developed an acronym for this: We should be "W-I-S-E" in all that we do. A chart of this is below:

Work Effort	Work hard in all that you do. Be dedicated to the mission and aligned with our clients' goals. We will meet or exceed their level of motivation and effort to accomplish all tasks assigned. Add extra to ordinary-be extraordinary.
Integrity	Do all things with integrity. Integrity means more than just honesty. It includes trustworthiness, reliability, and loyalty. We are dependable to deliver what we promise. We are truthful in all our words and actions.
Service	Have an attitude of servanthood. Our mission is to serve the needs of our clients and to do it with a cheerful attitude. We consider others better than ourselves. Always keep our clients' best interests at heart.
Expertise	Work not only hard but smart. Maximize the use of your talents for the benefit of our clients. Properly utilize the tools at hand. Be proactive. Measure the results and manage to expectations. Use "Best Practices."

This is not some incredibly newfound insight. These are the basics. If we put forth a solid, skillful effort done with integrity and cheerful service, we will be successful. Consider the various positive characteristics one associates with a Christian: caring, helpful, honest, and committed. You will find that these traits make one successful in the business world as well. They are a successful way of living life.

We should all work hard at whatever we do and remember whom we ultimately serve. "Whatever you do, work at it with all your heart, as working for the Lord, not for men, since you know that you will receive an inheritance from the Lord as a reward. It is the Lord Christ you are serving" (Col. 3:23–24 NIV). As an artist signs her paintings, every task we perform has our signature on it. We get to exclaim, "I did that." However, we may not want our signatures on some of the actions that we perform; we may not be proud of what we did. We should try to avoid these "works of art" and remember that we are working for the Lord in all that we do.

We should do all things with integrity. Integrity is more than just being honest. It includes trustworthiness, reliability, and loyalty. As the Good Book teaches, "I know, my God, that you examine our hearts and rejoice when you find integrity there" (1 Chron 29:17a NLT). "Integrity guides decent people, but hypocrisy leads treacherous people to ruin" (Prov 11:3 GWT). Not being reliable or loyal to the goals and the mission of any endeavor makes us undependable. Being deceitful makes us untrustworthy. In the consulting world, your name is all that you have. This is true for life in general. If our names are associated with dishonesty and deceit, then our names are useless. Therefore, we should be very careful to say what we mean and to deliver on what we promise.

We should do all things with skill and a cheerful heart. Peter writes, "God has given each of you a gift from His great variety of spiritual gifts. Use them well to serve one another" (1 Peter 4:10 NLT). We all have natural abilities and skills that we have developed over time through formal or informal training. We should apply those skills in such a manner to be the very best that we can be, and we should perform them with the right attitude—the attitude of servanthood.

At work, we often have tasks to complete that are then given to another person for them to perform their work to add value or enhance the product or service that the company is providing. Using Total Quality Management concepts, each person who receives our work is our "customer," and we should be mindful of providing excellent customer service. This concept is the same in dealing with our neighbor across the street. We should serve one another.

This attitude of servanthood applies to our leadership as well. When the disciples were arguing over who was going to sit next to Jesus during His reign in heaven, Jesus had to realign their priorities. He told them, "Those who are the greatest among you should take the lowest rank, and the leader should be like a servant" (Luke 22:26 NLT). To be a great leader you do not exalt yourself; instead, you humble yourself.

In this concept, you take your company's organizational chart and turn it upside down with the CEO at the bottom. This is truly how it works, for the CEO's job is to assist, enable, and instruct his or her subordinates so that they are the most effective and productive. They in turn do the same to their subordinates all the way to the workers at the top who are doing the work. The president of the United States is arguably the most powerful position in the whole world. The position is still classified as a civil servant because the ultimate goal should be that of serving the American people. Jesus even claimed that this leadership style applied to Himself—the ultimate King of kings and Lord of lords: "For even the Son of Man came not to be served but to serve others and to give His life as a ransom for many" (Matt. 20:28 NLT). If this wisdom leadership methodology applies to Jesus, it certainly applies to us.

Pastor Andy Stanley did a superb sermon series on wisdom entitled "Foolproof." He claims that whenever we face a decision, the greatest question to ask is, "What is the wise thing to do?" It's not, "What's the right thing," or "the best thing," or "how-much-can-I-get-away-with thing"; the greatest question is, "What is the *wise* thing to do?"

He goes on further to put it into this context: "In light of your past experiences, in view of your current circumstances, and in consideration of your future hopes and dreams, what is the wise thing to do?" We remember our past (sometimes too vividly), and we know where we have trouble. We can objectively evaluate our current situation in terms of work, finances, relationships, and so forth. We all have dreams, visions, and goals that we aspire to achieve. We should consider all these things when facing a decision, and *then* we should ask, "What is the wise thing to do?"

So how do we discern what the wise thing is? This is the tough part: We ask God for it. That seems too easy, but that's what James, the Lord's brother, tells us: "If any of you needs wisdom to know what you should do, you should ask God, and He will give it to you. God is generous to everyone and doesn't find fault with them" (James 1:5 GWT). James goes on to say in verse 6 (NLT): "But when you ask Him, be sure that your faith is in God alone. Do not waver, for a person with divided loyalty is as unsettled as a wave of the sea that is blown and tossed by the wind."

We must ask in faith, and it is a continual asking. We should ask for His wisdom to guide us in our decision-making each day. We must believe in God, believe that He is good, and believe that He will deliver on His promises. We cannot doubt this, nor can we ask out of ulterior motives. We trust in our Father that He will do what is best for us and guide us in the proper direction. How do we gain this faith and trust in Him? We get ourselves on a spiritual training program, as we discussed in the beginning of this chapter.

We've now come full circle, so let's review: If we have accepted Jesus Christ as our Lord and Savior, then we have chosen a life of discipleship. Being a disciple means being a student—to be a learner in a training program. Like any training program—physical, educational, or spiritual—it is a process. Like any process, there are good ways and better ways to follow. The better the quantity and quality of effort we put in, the better the results we will receive. It is quite unwise to profess a belief in Christ and then simply cascade along in life doing as we please until we get in such a jam that we find ourselves begging God to get us out of the mess we've made. Unfortunately, many of us try this training program, and very few are happy with the results. Life *is* tougher when we're stupid.

It is far better to be focused on our discipleship. Just like getting in good physical shape, it's sometimes hard to get off the couch and make it to the gym. Getting to the gym is the difficult part, but leaving the gym after the workout is easy. We are improving our health and condition, and we feel better, too. Studying is rarely on anyone's top-ten list of things to do, but having that knowledge in our head and applying it to our work or daily living brings satisfaction. Studying God's Word may seem like a chore at first, but as we grow, we'll have more of those "ah-ha" moments of spiritual insight. We will grow in wisdom. When we volunteer to help others, it may initially seem like an inconvenience, but when we understand the concept of being a blessing to others, we will be overwhelmed by the fulfillment it brings to our lives.

Getting started on a spiritual training program as a disciple of Christ may initially seem like a burden, but it will quickly become a blessing. When we are fully committed and fully immersed in the process (i.e. go "all in"), we will find that living a life for Christ is a blast! Now that is truly the wise thing to do and a lifestyle worth gaining.

35. A Sweet Fragrance

Jack Wehmiller

Every now and then a person has the opportunity to watch real heroes at work. More often than not, it is an ordinary person doing an extraordinary thing. The "hero" almost always doesn't even think that they are doing anything special. As a matter of fact, they seldom want any recognition for what they have just done. They were doing what they perceived as necessary. There is something internal in them that says, "If not now, when? If not me, who?"

I have had the privilege of witnessing just such events. Allow me to tell about two of them that took place recently. In less than thirty seconds on January 12, more than 250,000 people were killed in the Port-au-Prince area of Haiti. Twice that many were left homeless, hurt, and forever changed. We all heard about it. We all saw it on the news. We all had a choice as to how to respond. These are stories about how some did in fact respond. This is about people who said, "I will be the one who goes."

Wave after wave of doctors, nurses, and other first responders flowed into Haiti almost immediately. They arrived along with supplies at the airport, which was only a short walking distance from the triage area and the operating tents. These tents were as large as what we would see when the circus came to town, and the activity around them was at a feverish pitch. The Marines were guarding all supplies and all of the relief workers. People had come from all over the world to do what they could.

The carnage was unimaginable. For every medical professional who came there were at least 100 new patients. This Caribbean island, known as Hispaniola with two countries divided only by a mountain range was the site of what we would learn to be mankind at its finest. It was as we have read about in Corinthians. The sweet fragrance of Christ was shared by those that came to help.

While there are language barriers and cultural differences between the Dominican Republic and Haiti, there was no differentiation in the fact that all of them were God's children and many of them were hurt very badly. The Dominican side of the island felt the tremors but experienced no real damage. No buildings down, no death, only a feeling that something was terribly wrong just a short distance over the mountains.

First came the reports of the quake. Then came the flood of ambulances and other emergency vehicles into towns such as Barahona close to the border and Santo Domingo (the capital a full ten hours of driving away), bringing people who were simply in the wrong place at the wrong time. The initial wave of help came directly to Port-au-Prince, but soon the Haitians that had left their country were receiving help throughout the Dominican Republic. Many had the chance to see the very best of what we as human beings have to offer. Medical teams of surgeons landing at the site of the disaster began to operate in fifteen-hour shifts with little rest before the next grueling stretch of amputations and repairing of shattered limbs. This was more than just adrenaline pumping through their veins. This was far more special than that. As I stated earlier, it was greater than ordinary people doing extraordinary things. It was extraordinary people doing amazing things. It was humbling to watch—incredible to experience. As Paul Harvey would say, "But here is the rest of the story."

There were many who could not take vacation time and go immediately. Some were in school and couldn't leave that very day. In many cases they wanted to go, but just could not. In this situation in Haiti, the problem is so large that the need for help is going to last for decades. No one will be showing up too late to help.

Almost three months have passed, and Spring Break 2010 was upon us. As all of us know this is a big deal for young people in school. Fort Lauderdale and Panama City, Florida (better known to us in Georgia as the "Redneck Riviera"), are always on the hot list of places to go. I would venture to say that a poor community in the sugar cane fields just outside of Barahona, Dominican Republic, is not number three on the list of most college students looking for a relaxing destination in April. On my last trip to the island, I had been asked to assess medical and construction needs and report to several groups that wanted to go and do their part. One of those groups was a team of students from the Medical College of Augusta and a seasoned surgeon from Dalton, Georgia. It just so happened that the surgeon's daughter was one of those students. I gave them my report, and the trip was set for Easter weekend.

These students, I would come to find out, were very special. They brought military duffel bags full of medicine and supplies. They brought a wonderful enthusiasm. I am here to tell you that our future is brighter than what we have been told. There is a whole generation of humble, loving, and generous young people on the way to the fight. After a four-hour flight and a six-hour bus ride, we arrived at the Mission House in Barahona. The next day the twelve first- and second-year students and the doctor began their work with Haitian and Dominican families alike in what we know as Batey Seven. They were going to minister to both the physical and emotional needs of the "Invisible Poor." People they had never seen before and probably would never see again. And minister they did. I was not there for the entire trip, but I do know that on the first day, over 100 patients were seen.

Blood pressure problems were attended to, wounds were cared for, some minor surgery was done, and a tremendous amount of medicine was dispatched with love and caring. The best part came at the end of the day. We all walked around the village and played with the children. It was quite a crowd after going 100 yards or so. The kids were coming from every corner of the place. We had them riding on our backs; we were singing. It was glorious, just simply glorious. Twelve young people, a doctor, and myself, separated by a lot more than a plane flight and a bus ride—separated by more than lifestyle; but on that afternoon, we were all laughing in the same language. "The Twelve" were having the time of their lives, and I have no doubt that many of them will lead medical mission trips of their own in the near future.

I didn't witness what was done on the balance of this trip because I had meetings to attend back in the U.S. I do know that for good measure the team did some work on the construction of an orphanage that will house 105 youngsters when completed. We hear an awful lot about what is wrong with the world. There is an untold amount of murder and mayhem on the news every night. The political scene has many of us weary. We are treated to the sordid goings on in Hollywood each time we wait in line at the grocery store, but I want to remind us all that there still exists an innate goodness that keeps shining through when it is needed the most—an indomitable spirit that will not and cannot be suppressed. I saw it. I know that it exists.

I am reminded of a true story and think that I will close with it. There is a mountainside in the heart of France that has soil particularly conducive to growing lavender. The people seized on an economic possibility and built a factory further up the mountain. The men that worked in the factory each day had the sweet smell of lavender permeate their hair and clothing each and every day. The people in the village could not hear the whistle blow at the end of the work day, but as the workers arrived in the town each evening the sweet fragrance of the lavender went before them. The wives and children would actually recognize that their loved ones were home because of the fragrance in the air. There is a sign in a restaurant not far from where we live that says, "Everyone who walks through our doors makes us happy—some by arriving, some by leaving." Make the people you come in contact with happy because you arrived. Be a sweet fragrance.

36. The Call to Ministry

Emmett Holley

Now for the rest of "The News"

I already have one article in this book called *"The News"* that describes how I learned to let go and let God help me deal with a cancerous tumor in my left eye, which I eventually lost. This is a continuation of the story of my struggles and the trust that God was asking me to put in Him.

God calls us all into ministry—to be His witnesses for His Kingdom. From an earthly perspective, sometimes that call doesn't appear too glorious, and there are difficult moments when you sometimes wonder or had hoped that call was a wrong number. But God doesn't make mistakes, and if you can cling to Him and rest in Him, you will find a measure of joy and peace that goes beyond circumstances and human understanding.

When you tell God that you trust Him in all your ways, and you have given all of your plans to Him, He might test your faith. My life changed dramatically after losing my left eye to cancer. The physical challenge was mild in comparison to all of the questions that came from people who wanted to know what had happened. My old testimony, which of course bored most people to death, had to be refined into a new testimony concerning how I learned to love my Savior and trust

185

Him through a traumatic process. God taught me to share with others how He took my hand and guided me through my struggle, and this process taught me that I could trust Him in every encounter and every aspect of my life.

The following paragraphs will describe just how much He wanted me to trust Him. God opened the door for me to boldly be a witness to His miracle in keeping my cancer under control, and He showed me how He would help me to share with others how to let go of these kind of issues in all phases of life and to let Him take control.

Little did I know that God was not finished refining my testimony or testing my faith. I have been very fortunate to have great jobs for most of my life, and I give my thanks to God for that. I never finished college, I never had any special skills, and I certainly never deserved how much God blessed me from each of my jobs. With that being said, two years after I lost my eye to cancer, I lost my job as a construction manager. I loved the job and all of the people who worked with me, and it scared me to death to lose my job in my mid-forties with nothing to go into next.

Unfortunately, the construction industry was on a severe downturn in 2008, and that was my refuge to trying anything new. I prayed and prayed, and then I prayed some more. God allowed me to start my own business, and He blessed it in many ways. I met some wonderful people, and I was able to share my testimony with them. Unfortunately, the construction industry finally squeezed its last penny out of me after three years. My wife Ellen and I lost our home, and I managed to ruin our credit history in the process. I was on my knees begging God for His wisdom and knowledge because I didn't know what to do. I was unemployed except for a few small jobs, and I was barely making ends meet. I had to do what God told me to do: Trust Him in all of my ways, and He would take control. This trust is not easily transferrable to your family who is also being forced out of their comfortable home. Ellen and I looked for somewhere to rent and couldn't find anything. I knew that God would provide a place for us that we could afford. For many years, we had lived in a beautiful home that we designed ourselves, and it was in a wonderful neighborhood. It was not easy letting go of that and finding no place suitable to live.

Ellen struggled, and we cried together and separately about our situation. I had mentioned to Ellen that she might call an organization in our church called Stephen Ministry just to talk with someone. She spoke with Nancy Page, who was one of the leaders of the Stephen Ministry. Ellen's original plan was to arrange for someone to talk with, and nothing more. After their conversation ended, Nancy said, "We have a place to rent." I was working on a small job in Atlanta on a Saturday afternoon when I got a call from Ellen. Ellen told me about the home that Nancy had for us to rent, but after looking at it, she thought that it would be more than we could afford. I told Ellen that God would provide, and He did. The rent was well within our budget. I fell on my knees and praised God for his provision. I trusted Him and fell a little deeper in love with Him.

When my small construction business finally met its end, I found myself looking for another industry—I would do and learn anything to have a steady job. Before the construction industry, I had worked in a factory for eleven years for a company that made piston rings for diesel trucks. I had management skills and received great training in both the construction industry and the industrial manufacturing environment. I had no certificates or degrees to speak of, and I knew that finding work after my company ended would not be an easy task. However, I knew that God wouldn't let my family and me down. He had a plan.

I gave my resume to anyone and everyone just hoping that I would get a call. No calls came, and I will admit that I was getting a little frustrated with God. A small, tender voice kept saying, "Trust Me." I revisited all of the employment offices just to make sure that they hadn't lost my information, and to adjust my salary requirements to whatever an employer was willing to pay me. I knew that God would provide for my needs. "We have nothing" was the overwhelming response.

After driving around and submitting resumes for any job, I was becoming desperate. During one of my employment excursions, I was hungry and wanted to stop to get something to eat, but I didn't have very much money. When I had been in similar situations before, I had headed for the Dollar Store. I knew that I could get something to eat for one dollar if I had to. When I approached the counter to pay for my lunch, I noticed a man standing there who I recognized but didn't know from where I remembered him. When you get older, that becomes the norm. You remember the face but not the name. Curiosity finally got the best of me, and I asked the gentlemen, "I know you from somewhere; what is your name?"

He said, "Dex Smith." Then we remembered that we had worked together in the piston ring business; he had been my supervisor. We shook hands and shared what God had done in our lives over the years. I asked him if he knew of any place that was hiring, and his immediate response was yes. I was getting pretty excited at this point. Dex had been working for an industrial plastic molding business and had received a promotion, and they were looking to replace him. He knew my experience and my work ethic, and thought that I could get a job at his company. He even called the human resources office to let them know I was looking for a job, and he recommended me.

God was working on a plan.

Ironically, it happened at the Dollar Store. I remember sitting in the parking lot after that conversation crying and praising God for such a wonderful encounter. I interviewed for the position, and they offered me a job as a machine worker on third shift. It would be a temporary position until I was deemed capable of doing the job. After the interim period had ended, I was not only offered a job, but it was on the second shift as a team manager, which of course meant more dollars per hour. God had a plan.

I liked my new position, and even though the hours were long and I didn't get to see my wife much, I knew that God would somehow work it out. The company was growing in every direction, and I knew that it would only be a matter of time before I would be on the day shift. I was doing great, working hard, and losing weight, which I attributed to working so many hours.

I started to get a little concerned about my weight loss, and Ellen noticed a spot on the left side of my jaw that was swollen. This time, I didn't wait to go see the doctor as I had done with my eye; I made the appointment quickly. One night after work, I came home with a terrible backache that overwhelmed me. I told Ellen that the pain was too severe to ignore, and we needed to go to the hospital. I needed something to help with the pain, and I needed it right then. After doing the X-ray on my back, the doctor told us that we needed to make an appointment with my doctor because there were some abnormalities in my back. We had already been to see the doctor previously over my concerns with the weight loss and the lump under my jaw. The doctor knew my previous experience with cancer and ordered the appropriate test to be done. We didn't hear anything from the doctor for about two weeks and were starting to get a little worried.

Then the call came.

"Emmett, you have an appointment this Friday, and you and your wife need to come." When we sat down to talk with the doctor, I could tell that something was wrong. He very quickly said, "Emmett, I am sorry to tell you that your cancer is back, and it's all throughout your body. You have stage 4 metastatic cancer." Thank God that Ellen was there with me, as we were both in shock. I asked the doctor if anything could be done. He told us that without treatment I had maybe three to six months to live, and with treatment, maybe a year. As the tears started streaming down Ellen's face, I heard the same voice that I have heard so many times in my life say, "I have you, Emmett." It was God reassuring me that along with everything else, this was under His control, too. Instead of tears, He put a smile on my face. I knew that I was in His hands, and He would be leading us on this new journey.

Through His gracious and wonderful love, God reminded of what He had told me the first time cancer called: "Emmett, everything will be all right, whether I take you to your home or mine."

Due to my diagnosis, my immediate response was to resign my position at work and spend the rest of my time with my family. I didn't know how much time I had left, but I wanted to take care of a few things so that Ellen wouldn't have to when God was ready to take me home. I sat down with my employer and told them what a wonderful experience I had working for them, and how much I appreciated them giving me a position in their company, but I didn't have much of a choice in this job. I didn't think that I'd had enough time working there to receive any kind of benefits if I left. I knew that God would somehow provide through His infinite wisdom. On my way home after resigning, I received a phone call from the human resources administrator. She said, "Emmett, this is Pam; you qualified for disability by one week."

Once again, I cried and praised God for His wonderful love for me and His provision for all of my needs. It wasn't as much money as I was making, but it was certainly going to be an easier road financially. I never missed a paycheck. Imagine this: When I attained this employment, I put together a budget of what we would need in addition to Ellen's income. The amount was based on what I was earning per hour when I first started in my new position as a machine operator. Amazingly enough, the amount I would receive in disability benefits was exactly what we needed plus some. God had foreseen my needs and already made provision. God had a plan already in place.

As you can imagine, we had no inclination as to what or where this new journey would take us. We were in God's hands, and He would direct our new path in His time frame. The first part of our journey took us to the oncologist who qualified the original diagnosis. He scheduled immediate and radical chemotherapy in response to the amount of cancer in my body. After our appointment with the oncologist, he called us during the next week and said that before we started the chemotherapy, I needed to have an MRI (magnetic resonance image) of my brain. He followed through with his recommendation and scheduled the MRI.

After having the MRI completed, I received another call.

It was from the oncologist, and he said, "Emmett, I have some bad news for you. You have multiple tumors in your brain, and before we start any kind of chemotherapy, we need to try and treat your brain tumors." I found it kind of funny that he said that he had more bad news for me. I had just been told I had three to six months to live without treatment—maybe a year with treatment. What kind of bad news was there in addition to that?

The next part of our journey took Ellen and me to a radio oncologist who also informed us that he had counted at least twenty tumors in my brain, and then he had stopped counting. The radio oncologist scheduled radiation treatments immediately. The schedule was to give as much radiation to my brain as it could stand in an attempt to kill or delay the growth of the tumors in my brain. Ellen and I stood strong in our faith in God just as we had through the journey thus far.

We returned to our chemical oncologist after four weeks to learn the results of the MRI. The treatments had not worked, and additional tumors had grown since the original scan. This was not very good news. However, we knew that Jesus said we are healed by His stripes, and we claimed that for me.

We never lost our faith in God or our trust in His path. I was originally diagnosed on September 23, 2011, and my appointment schedule was once per month. I was given a powerful steroid to limit the growth of the tumors and a plethora of other drugs to counteract the use of the steroid. The cancer began to impact me physically due to the tumors in my spine. I slowly lost my ability to walk without a walker. Over the next few months, I lost my ability to walk with a walker. I had been attending a men's Bible study with help from my best friend, Tom McAllister, who by the way is the guy who made it possible for me to share my story in this book. I asked the guys in our study to pray for God's help with my search for a wheelchair. In the same study, my brothers in Christ placed their hands on my head and shoulders and prayed for God's healing for me. In the afternoon of the same day, I received a surprise visit from Doug Hansen, another best friend and a contributor of a couple of stories in this book. He delivered a wheelchair to me. God has a plan, and my love for Him is growing stronger through every situation.

My testimony was increasing through this journey as I experienced God's amazing love and saw the many ways He was using me through my affliction. Now all I needed was a wheelchair ramp. I planned it to the detail, but God had a different plan.

Much to my surprise, a stack of lumber appeared in my front yard. The next day Nick Delozier and his dad Don Delozier, along with Jim Johnson and Larry Vandiver appeared at my home at around 4:00 p.m. I had worked with all of these men in my construction career. My wheelchair ramp was completed by 10:00 p.m. that night. They were unbelievable and awesome. God's plan was better than mine. The next week, my paralysis had progressed so that I could no longer walk at all. I was now confined completely to the use of the wheelchair. If I had gone by my plan, my wheelchair ramp would have not been completed for two months.

In addition, Tom and I were able to complete a fence in the backyard to accommodate our dogs Sarah and Gracie. Although they are both indoor dogs and 95 percent potty trained, we would take them for walks morning and evening to relieve them of any pressures they might have accumulated during the day. Now that Daddy was home with them all the time, the pups thought that Dad and his wheelchair could continue to walk them. Although this is not possible, now I can just open the door and let them out.

Throughout this journey, I have received numerous cards and emails of love and support. They have all brought me inspiration and encouragement. Many people have prayed for me, and I was able to blog my status on a wonderful website called Caring Bridge. Since the radiation didn't work, there was no need for me to do chemotherapy, as it was assumed that the brain tumors would eventually cause my demise. So I took my steroids and other drugs, and I started taking lots of the nutritional supplement Reliv that Tom's friend Marcia, another contributing author in this book, recommended. I continued to see the oncologist, and we both recognized that I didn't seem to be showing any signs of brain tumors. He asked if I was willing to have some scans done to see what was going on. We scheduled the scans and made an appointment to see the oncologist after the scans.

A couple of days later, the phone rang.

This time it was just a telemarketer—false alarm.

We went to the doctor's office for our appointment, and when the oncologist came into the room, he informed us that the tumors were resolved. I asked him what that meant, and he told us that it meant that the tumors were gone. Can you say divine intervention? The doctor said that the radiation treatment sometimes takes a while before any kind of improvement can be seen. In my now tumor-free mind, I was thinking there is a big difference between a decrease in size of the tumors and a disappearance of the tumors altogether.

God had a plan, and my testimony to His amazing love was increased again.

We decided to schedule chemotherapy to help with the other tumors in my lungs and my bones. The initial treatments were bearable; however, as the treatments continued, my quality of life decreased significantly. Ellen and I prayed fervently and decided that I would not have any additional treatments. God had provided for our every need throughout this journey, and we would listen for His word and follow His plans.

It is now November 21, 2013, twenty-seven months from the original diagnosis. God is not finished with me. He loves me, and

I love Him more and more. I wake up thanking Him for every new day. I thank Him for my struggles and for His strength through these struggles. God has challenged me to show His Love to everyone I meet. He is keeping me around to finish the job. When I have witnessed to the last person that He wants me to witness to, He will take me home.

I want to conclude with my favorite verse of scripture. It sustains me through all my endeavors.

"Trust God from the bottom of your heart; don't try and figure out everything on your own. Listen for God's voice in everything you do; everywhere you go; He's the one that will keep you on track" (Proverbs 3:5–6 MSG).

May we all stay on track by putting our complete trust in God.

37. Theory of Relativity

Tom McAllister

In 1905 Albert Einstein introduced to the world his theory of special relativity. The centerpiece of his work revolved around the famous equation:

$$E = mc^2$$

Where **E** represents Energy, **m** represents Mass, and **c** is a Constant (the speed of light in a vacuum, which is approximately 186,000 miles/second).

Though mathematically simplistic in form, the implications were extremely complex. Special relativity introduces the concept of unifying space and time in a continuum called space-time. It revealed that time itself was not constant but varied dependent upon the speed of the traveling mass. You have to be really smart or using very strong hallucinogens to come up with something like that. The main accomplishment of the theory was that it established a relationship between two distinct entities: energy and mass.

Although the mathematical aspects of the equation are not fully analogous, we can use this equation to illustrate relationships in the spiritual realm. There is a relationship between the Creator (God) and His created (mankind). In the beginning, this relationship was a direct connection. Man had a sinless nature and could come into the presence of Almighty God. Adam and Eve enjoyed the Garden of Eden and all its delights with no deadlines or drama. Life was a party! Considering their attire, God's initial plans for us were to *party naked.* How's that for a cool Creator? Then humankind stumbled and sinned, and this special relationship was immediately severed. God, perfect and holy, cannot be "connected" to anything unholy. Even the slightest blemish prevents such a connection, for God's absolute holiness requires zero defects. To be perfectly holy, everything must be perfectly holy. This was not good news for humankind, as we were now separated from God. Thus, when Adam and Eve sinned, they suffered instant spiritual death and separation from God. This corruption infected their physical bodies as well, and they began to age and eventually die. This "infection" of sin has been passed down from our first couple, Adam and Eve, to every human being ever born. We are all seeds from Adam, and like begets like. We all share this sinful nature. God demands perfection, and we cannot deliver. He does not grade on a curve. Even if we were like Ivory soap and were 99 and 44/100ths percent pure, we still wouldn't make the cut.

Fortunately for us, nothing surprises God, and long before the first humans sinned, He already had a plan to resolve this dreadful dilemma. His solution is perhaps the most inspiring verse in the Bible: "For God so loved the world that He gave His only begotten Son, that whoever believes in Him shall not perish, but have eternal life" (John 3:16 NASB).

God is Spirit (John 4:24). He is the Source; He is the Energy (E) that created all things. To restore the relationship and balance in the equation with mankind (m), God had to add (C); He had to add Christ. When we as individuals accept Christ as our Savior, then we are made righteous in God's eyes, and there is no condemnation for those in Christ Jesus (Rom. 8:1). When we receive Christ, we receive His Spirit, the Holy Spirit in us. The combination of man in Christ through the

Holy Spirit (mC^2) is acceptable by God; the equation balances, for we have infinite holiness on both sides, and our relationship with Him is restored. When God looks at us, He does not regard our sinful nature. He sees Christ in us. He sees the righteousness of Christ in us, and He smiles and says, "That's my Boy!"

So how does this relationship work? How do we relate to this creative, personal Force, this Spirit we call God the Father; to His Son, Jesus Christ; and to the Holy Spirit—one God in three Persons? The mystery of the Trinity is beyond my "blue collar" faith level to explain in detail. Some analogies of the Holy Trinity compare it to water: Water exists in three phases—water, steam, and ice, but they all are the same H_2O molecule. Similarly, God is one Entity in three forms. Another description is that Christ and the Holy Spirit are the Hands of God the Father working in our lives. Complete comprehension of the Trinity is beyond the current capability of humankind. However, God has described in detail in His Word how this relationship between the triune God and humankind is to work.

The first step is to gain the proper perspective. We should have an attitude of complete reverence toward God. It's not a peer relationship. We are the created; He is our Creator. He is all powerful; He merely spoke this entire magnificent universe into existence! When we see the beauty of nature, witness the intricacies of how the universe operates, and experience the miracle of childbirth, we get a glimpse of how wonderful God is. He knows each of us down to the last atom of our bodies, and He loves us with a love so great that it is beyond our measure. Knowing this should inspire us to worship Him in absolute awe and wonder. He is so big, and we are so small. Yet, He is a perfect Father Who loves us and wants to mentor us, and He is leading us on the best possible path for our lives. We can trust Him completely, and by trusting in Him, we can love Him. If we love Him, then we'll want to obey Him.

The other key aspects are similar to those required in any successful relationship: honesty, sound communication, and commitment, all held together in love. We cannot have a relationship without communicating, and there is no point in communicating if we're going to lie. Likewise, no relationship will last without the commitment to maintain it. We communicate to God through prayer and worship. He communicates to us through His Word, through others, and directly into our hearts. The more involved the dialogue, the closer the relationship becomes. "Draw near to God and He will draw near to you" (James 4:8 NASB). Honesty with God is accomplished through a pure heart. "Blessed are the pure in heart for they will see God" (Matt. 5:8 NIV). Having a pure heart does not mean having a perfect heart. A pure heart is an honest heart. It's saying, "Here I am, Lord, the good, the bad, and the ugly." God made us, and He knows us better than we know ourselves. He knows our strengths and weaknesses. We cannot keep secrets from God, so why should we try? He knows all our thoughts anyway. We should just be ourselves. We commit ourselves to God by living our lives for Him in love. "Love means doing what God has commanded us, and He has commanded us to love one another, just as you heard from the beginning" (2 John 1:6 NLT). God is committed to us in that He gave up His Son to die for us so that we may have a relationship with Him. "The LORD Himself goes before you and will be with you; He will never leave you nor forsake you. Do not be afraid; do not be discouraged" (Deut. 31:8 NIV). God's commitment to you is unquestionable.

If we have difficulty in fully grasping this, we can look to His Son. He is the true image of God in human form. Jesus even said, "...whoever has seen Me, has seen the Father" (John 14:9). Not only is Jesus our Lord and Savior, He is our benchmark in how we are to live. Jesus lived a sinless life, and therefore He was truthful in all that He did. He is Truth. He was in constant communication with the Father in thought and prayer. He fully submitted to the Father's will for His life, even unto death on a cross. As we follow God and grow in Christ, we become more Christ-like. As a branch grows and looks more like the vine, we also grow in our spiritual life and become more like Him.

We further enhance our relationship with God through our relationships with others. At first glance, this logically appears secondary, but God gives it equal weight. When Jesus was asked, "What is the greatest commandment?" He replied, "You shall love the Lord your God with all your heart and with all your soul and with all your mind. This is the great and first commandment. And a second is like it: You shall love your neighbor as yourself. On these two commandments depend all the Law and the Prophets" (Matt. 22:37–40 ESV). In a sound bite, loving your neighbor is simply following the Golden Rule of treating others with kindness and respect just as we wish to be treated with kindness and respect. As we grow in our relationship with God the Father, we will recognize His abounding love and grace and want to share it with others. We are His witnesses to share the Gospel and encourage others to become His disciples—students of the Word and followers of Christ.

We therefore demonstrate our love for God not only through obedience and worship, but also in how we relate to others. God truly cares how we treat all others, not just how we treat our friends. In His last meal with His disciples, Jesus told them, "A new commandment I give to you, that you love one another: just as I have loved you, you also are to love one another. By this all people will know that you are my disciples, if you have love for one another" (John 13:34–35 ESV). People will recognize you by how you behave and treat others. When you are showing them caring respect and love, they will know that you are one of God's children.

Finally, we should recognize what it means to be a child of God. You are a child of the King. Therefore, you are a prince or princess! Most of us tend to behave in a certain manner based on the different groups, associations, or organizations in which we participate. These memberships become part of our identity. When we hang out with our peers and colleagues in the business world, many of us try to act sophisticated and professional. For those in school, jocks behave differently from those in the Chess Club, who act differently from the cheerleading squad, who relate differently from those in the band, and so on. People who drive trucks, have tattoos, enjoy similar hobbies, support the same sports teams, or share any sort of common bond develop an affinity and often behave in a manner that is typical for that social group, be it formal or informal. It's an innate desire within us to belong to a particular group.

As Christians, we belong to the body of Christ. We are part of the family of God and are heirs to His kingdom. We should act like children of royalty. This does not mean to act with the arrogance of entitlement. We're His children by His grace—we did nothing to earn it. We should be humbled by that fact, immeasurably appreciative of His mercy, and we should behave in righteousness through our obedience to our Father the King. The apostle Paul described it this way:

> So if you're serious about living this new resurrection life with Christ, act like it. Pursue the things over which Christ presides. Don't shuffle along, eyes to the ground, absorbed with the things right in front of you. Look up, and be alert to what is going on around Christ—that's where the action is. See things from His perspective (Col. 3:1–2 MSG).

It's a perspective of royalty. It's good to be a child of the King, and this relationship matters most of all. You have the greatest Dad there is, and the benefits to being His child far exceed everything else. It's truly the greatest way to live. You don't have to be an Einstein to figure that out.

38. Sun Down

Tom McAllister

In the business world, bad news doesn't improve with age. In the medical field, an untreated wound will fester. In the restaurant business, dirty dishes will not wash themselves. As a former owner and partner in a barbecue restaurant (now this is North Carolina-style barbecue, so we're talking *gourmet 'cue* here), I was amazed at how fast dirty dishes can pile up.

It's funny, but that latter rule applies at home, too. As a bachelor, I have a significantly higher threshold and tolerance for dirty dishes than most, as I nonchalantly observe their sprawl across the kitchen counter. However, I will personally attest that there's a price to be paid for it. Have you ever left a cereal bowl with a few corn flakes left in it for several days in a sink? What could have easily been rinsed out with a quick squirt of water now takes an immense amount of effort of soaking, scrubbing, and sometimes scraping with a knife or other sharp object. Gorilla Glue doesn't hold as strong as a six-day cured, dried piece of cereal on the side of a bowl. What could have been solved quickly in the beginning now takes considerable effort after a completely avoidable, sloth-induced delay.

This "parable of the stubborn cornflake" especially applies to relationships in conflict.

When we get into a conflict with another person, the immediate reaction for the majority of us is to go the other way or leave it alone. Most of us are conflict avoiders. There are some who enjoy conflict and initiate it, but that approach is like trying to douse a flame with gasoline. However, the path of least resistance is to let things go, hope they simmer down, and, like those dirty dishes, hope that they somehow miraculously get washed.

That's not a wise approach. Yes, if we become so angry that we've lost control of our emotions, we must first regain our composure. But as soon as we do, we must begin the reconciliation process. The longer we wait, the more that emotional wound will fester and the harder that "cornflake of distrust" will become attached.

In Ephesians, Paul–another bachelor, incidentally—addresses the importance of this sort of spiritual housekeeping: "Don't sin by letting anger control you. Don't let the sun go down while you are still angry, for anger gives a foothold to the devil" (Eph. 4:26-27 NLT).

There you go. The last thing we need to exacerbate a relationship problem is to allow the devil to assist in the counseling. He's always willing to give advice. It may be "pointed," but it's never cleansing. He thrives on conflict and he'll try to harden your heart like a two-week cured cornflake.

Yes, resolving conflict is challenging, and it is often more difficult with people that we really care about. The more we care, the more intense the emotion, and the more investment we have in jeopardy. But we have got to do it and do it quick. How important is this? *Very*. It is so important, look how Jesus described it.

> "Therefore if you are presenting your offering at the altar, and there remember that your brother has something against you, leave your offering there before the altar and go; first be reconciled to your brother, and then come and present your offering" (Matt. 5:23–24 NIV).

Our brother in this example might be our blood sibling or it could mean anyone. Now think carefully about this for a moment. This is Jesus talking about us giving our gift to God the Father Almighty. God, the Creator of the whole universe, Who deserves all glory, all honor and first priority in everything, wants us to delay our offering to Him and *first* be reconciled with the one with whom we have a disagreement.

Wow! If it's that important to Him, then it should be that important to us. God, fully wise and omniscient knows that the longer you wait, the worse it will get. This is not a suggestion (God never suggests)—it's a command. "Go and reconcile with the one with whom you have a disagreement. Then make your offering to Me."

My parents were married for fifty-five years before my dad went to be with the Lord. I asked my mom one day what were the keys to their marital success. One thing she said was that they made a commitment to never go to bed angry at each other. If there was a conflict, they stayed up all night if necessary until the path toward reconciliation had been established.

Some situations may not be resolved in one night, and we can't control the actions of the other party, but we need to make sure before the day is done that our "brother" knows that we have left the door of reconciliation propped wide open. We have initiated our part, and we must continue to speak the truth in love until the dispute is resolved. Like those unwashed dishes, it may be a dirty business, but the sooner we get started, the sooner the stubborn cornflake is removed and the sooner life will start cooking again in the cleaned kitchen of our relationship.

39. Follow to the Letter

Tom McAllister

Dear Nephew:

How be-ist thee? I hope you are bear-and-snake free and are enjoying your time in the California mountain wilderness. It's a cool opportunity that you have spending the summer camping and keeping hiking tourists safe up in the mountains, although I am sure that it gets a little lonesome. Not everyone is cut out to be a hermit.

So, since you have some time on your hands, I wanted to put together something for you to ponder as you pursue your career and your path in life. It gets very philosophical and theological, so it may take a few readings over time to absorb it all. It's more theory than pragmatic practice, but hopefully it will be helpful in establishing some life rules and principles that can guide you in your decision making as you venture into the world.

We start with this question: "What's the ultimate goal of a human life?" It's one of those mountaintop types of ponderings. Can it even be defined in universal terms, or is each life so unique that a particular path, goal, or methodology cannot be ascribed? We only have one life to live, and it gets closer to ending with each passing second, so it behooves all of us, wherever we are in life, to plot the proper course and develop an optimum strategy to live life to the fullest to achieve the maximum benefit to ourselves.

One could state that every person desires success. This is true, but then we come back to the crossroads of what the definition of success is. The answer is almost as unique as each individual is.

An appropriate metaphor for life is a journey, for life has many twists and turns, hills and valleys, smooth pavement, potholes, and an occasional Bridge Out Ahead sign. Sometimes you go off-road, and sometimes you even end up in a ditch, which is rarely an optimal place to be—and that is spoken from personal experience. If we use this metaphor and try to define the best way to travel, then perhaps we can develop a winning strategy for living a successful life.

Like any journey or trip, there are a few fundamental principles to successful travel. First, you have to know where you are going; next, you should pack the correct things and have the proper attitude during the trip; finally, there are certain "best practices" for your method of travel that will maximize your enjoyment and fulfillment along the way. I call these concepts the five Ps of successful travel, which I'll discuss shortly. Though the analogy of a physical trip is quite appropriate, this is referring to a spiritual journey, which is the most important journey you will ever take in life.

Every person's ultimate goal should be to find fulfillment in his or her life. People pursue many different paths and many different objectives to find this fulfillment. The famous French philosopher Blaise Pascal once wrote, "All men seek happiness. This is without exception. Whatever different means they employ, they all tend to this end...they will never take the least step but to this object. This is the motive of every action, of every man, even those who hang themselves."

Whether it is happiness (a rather superficial pursuit), or joy, or fulfillment, to use a more generic definition of being a success in all that you do, one certainly shouldn't get "hung up" in pursuing it, as that's definitely not a "Best Practice" solution!

But what should you pursue?

The world in which we live promotes a different value system than what Jesus taught. The world promotes wealth and fame as pinnacles of success. Television shows such as *Who Wants to Be a Millionaire?* and *American Idol* capture the world's attention. Wealth, power, beauty, and influence are the success metrics of the world system. Thus, the ultimate measure of success in the world would be someone who is so rich and powerful that he or she lends money to Bill Gates out of the petty cash fund. This person has warehouses full of trophies and personal awards such that his or her name dominates the achievements in the *Guinness Book of World Records*. The paparazzi constantly track this person's movements to provide continual updates to an infatuated public, members of the opposite sex swoon at their appearance (and nowadays maybe a few of the same sex), and this remarkable individual is atop everyone's "A" list and is worshipped and idolized by all. That doesn't sound too shabby, huh?

If there were no God, then this *would* be the definition of success. Make the most of your life; eat, drink and be merry, for one day you will die, and it will all be over.

Since there is a God, the scorecard is different. Certainly worldly achievements and accomplishments are worthwhile and should be acknowledged. Wealth, influence, and fame are enablers to greater opportunities, but in the end, they're irrelevant. Although people strongly desire and aspire to get on the celebrity "A" list, a better goal would be to get on the "G" list—God's list. The Book of Life is where you want your name to be. That's where it's happening—that's the best party in the whole universe, and the cool thing about it is that the fun lasts for all eternity. In a nutshell, this is *the Answer*.

In the consulting world, we talk about "best practices" or the right way to do things based on certain principles and experience. This concept applies to every activity in life. For a simple example, when you cross the street, "best practices" advise you to look both ways before crossing. To enhance this further, we should look left, then right, and then left again as we cross the street. In England, you do the opposite sequence since traffic flow is reversed. I think you get the picture. The biblical word for best practices is wisdom, and wisdom comes from God. "The fear of the LORD is the beginning of wisdom: and knowledge of the Holy One is understanding" (Prov. 9:10 ERV). In any situation that you face, ask yourself one question: What is the wise thing to do? The answer will help you choose the right path: The wisest thing to do is the will of God.

So in this journey of life, the best-practices method is to do the will of God. Jesus said, "Follow Me," so there's your path. He is the Way. To elaborate on this concept, just apply these Five-P principles while continually evaluating your situation and asking what the wise thing to do is. If you do this, then you will make sound choices and avoid tragedy and missteps along your journey.

So here goes. The five Ps are Priority, Perspective, Potential, Process, and Preparedness. These relate to a journey, in that you need to know where you are going, what attitude to have, how to make the most of the journey, the best way to travel, and how to pack for the trip.

Technically, you need to pack or be prepared before you start your journey. However, you must know where you are going and how you plan to get there before you know what to pack. You don't take your wool coat when you're headed to the beach, so we'll call the Preparedness P a prerequisite P.

Since you are an Eagle Scout, you understand the importance of being prepared. This should be a fundamental part of your mindset in everything you do. The appropriate verse is Ephesians 6:11 (NIV): "Put on the full armor of God so that you can take your stand against the devil's schemes." Why do we need to do this? "For our struggle is not against flesh and blood, but against the rulers, against the authorities, against the powers of this dark world and against the spiritual forces of evil in the Heavenly realms" (Eph. 6:12 NIV).

It's a dangerous world out there, so "be clear-minded and alert. Your opponent, the devil, is prowling around like a roaring lion, looking for someone to devour" (1 Peter 5:8 NIV). The twelve points of the Scout Law are character traits. Just as an athlete develops a skill such as hitting a baseball or throwing a football, these traits become the tools in your "backpack" to use in appropriate situations. When you act with courtesy and have an attitude of kindness, helpfulness, and cheerfulness, then you interact with the world through a positive message of respect and love. When you are trustworthy, loyal, thrifty, and obedient, you demonstrate self-discipline to sound principles of integrity that should not be compromised. When you are reverent, you acknowledge through your worship your Heavenly Father. He is the Creator of all, and as such, He is entitled to all glory and honor.

Just as you do when you're going out on the camping trail, you must be wearing the proper equipment. Using a sports analogy, a football player would be very unwise to run onto the field without his helmet on, even if he has a very hard head. So too you should not venture forth without all your equipment. Paul talks about all of these in Ephesians 6, but I'll review just a few of them.

Put on the helmet of salvation. The helmet protects the head, and the head leads the body. This is the most critical of all, for without salvation, nothing else matters. If you were to accomplish the ultimate in worldly success as described previously, yet did not have salvation through Jesus Christ, your life would be a total loss because it profits a person nothing if he gains the whole world and loses his soul (Mark 8:36).

The next piece of equipment is the breastplate of righteousness. The breastplate protects the heart, which is the dwelling place of the Holy Spirit. The condition of our spiritual heart is how God evaluates us. God sees not as man sees. God looks at the heart (1 Samuel 16:7). Keeping your heart pure and righteous enables God to work His purpose through you. I'll talk more about this in a moment.

The last two pieces I want to discuss are the shield of faith and the sword of the Spirit. You are protected by your faith in the promises of God's sufficient grace and mercy and in His Son's death and resurrection. Through faith, you know that you will never be tested beyond your capacity to handle it (1 Cor. 10:13).

Last is the sword of the Spirit or the Word of God. The sword is both an offensive and a defensive weapon. The Word of God is Truth. Remember, even the smallest truth can defeat the biggest lie, and our adversary is the devil who is the father of lies (John 8:44), so resist him through your knowledge of the Word with the sword of the Spirit, and he will flee from you (James 4:7). It is far more effective than bear repellent. (I hope you never have to use that.) This will prepare you well for your journey.

Now for the travel Ps: The first P is Priority. As in any journey, you must first know where you are going or else you will wind up lost or wasting time going to worthless, dead-end places. As the mouse in the maze would say, "There's no cheese down this tunnel." Life is a journey, and we should add that it is best traveled with a destination in mind. We need to know where we are going, not just in the ultimate sense of heaven, although that applies, but to travel our life's journey according to God's purpose and destination for us.

The appropriate scripture is Matthew 6:33: "Seek God's Kingdom first, and His righteousness, and all these things [that you need] will be provided unto to you." Note that we should seek God's Kingdom *first*. We're not to seek it *sometime during life*, or put it somewhere on our bucket list: See the Grand Canyon, get married, make a million dollars, and seek God's Kingdom. No, we're to pursue it with the absolute highest priority. Seeking His Kingdom first is like putting on a pair of godly glasses behind our eyes so that we can see the world from His "eternal" viewpoint. God's perspective and priority differ from the world's, so we must navigate through this life using His GPS system—call it God's Providence System. How important is this? It's our top priority.

Jesus told several parables about the Kingdom of God, and a couple of quickies are found starting in Mathew 13:44, where the Kingdom of God (or Heaven) is like a treasure found in a field or like a pearl of great value. When you read these parables, note the response of the person who discovered the treasure. He sold all that he had in order to obtain it. In other words, the Kingdom of God is worth all you got. So seek His Kingdom first and His righteousness, and always remember that it is His righteousness, not ours, that we seek and aspire to live by through obedient love. In response, God promises to provide all that we need. It may not be all that we think we want, but it will be all that we need to have a successful journey.

The second P is Perspective. This is the proper attitude for our journey. The appropriate scripture is Proverbs 3:5–6 (NIV): "Trust in the Lord with all your heart, and lean not on your own understanding. In all your works and all your ways acknowledge Him, and He will direct your path." Several things happen when we put our wholehearted trust in Him. First, it gives us confidence, for God will direct our path in the way we are to go. When you are walking along the path that God has set before you, you cannot improve upon your journey. Think about that for a moment. If you are in God's will and following God's path for you, it's like an Old Milwaukee commercial; it doesn't get any better than this. Perhaps I shouldn't reference a beer commercial, but it fits so nicely. God has a plan for all of us, and we can never say, "You know, God, that's not a bad way to go, but I've got a better idea." God is perfect, His plan is perfect, and when we're in the center of the fairway of His plan, we are right where we need to be.

The second thing this gives us is peace of mind. If we're right where God wants us to be, then we don't have to worry about anything, as we have that peace of mind that passes all understanding (Philippians 4:7). This peace of mind enables us to be environmentally independent, which is a great frame of mind to have in dealing with the trials and tribulations of life. When we trust God with all of our hearts, and

He is directing our path, then we can walk with total confidence and enjoy the fruits of the Spirit in any situation: love, joy, peace, patience, and kindness (Galatians 5:22). We can be happy with a lot or a little, be in a palace or a prison, and this peace of mind will enable us to not only endure whatever circumstance we are in—even if we're alone atop a mountain being harassed by mosquitoes—but we can do so singing praises to God (see Acts 16:25).

The third P is Potential. Like the Army, we should be all that we can be in our journey throughout life. Our objective in life is to fulfill the purpose that God has planned for us. God guides us through our hearts. Matthew 5:8 states, "Blessed are the pure in heart for they shall see God." There is a direct correlation between our purity of heart and God's ability to direct us for His purpose. If our heart is only partially pure, He can use us only partially. A pure heart is not a perfect heart. None of us has a perfect heart, for we all have sinned and fallen short of the glory of God (Rom. 3:23). A pure heart is simply an honest heart. God seeks a relationship with us, and, as in all relationships, it requires honesty to operate effectively. We are to be open and honest with Him. We are to tell Him of all our thoughts, hopes, dreams, and fears with brutal honesty. He knows them already, but He wants us to relate to Him with complete integrity—to come to Him with a pure heart. We are to trust Him with our whole heart, and we are to be honest with Him: "Here I am, Lord, warts, imperfections, and all." We can be angry, sad, hurt, or happy, and it's okay with God. Our integrity is what counts.

This particular verse is from the Sermon on the Mount where Jesus makes several encouraging statements of blessing. When you read these, some seem more beneficial, such as "blessed are the merciful, for they shall receive mercy," or "blessed are the meek, for they shall inherit the earth." Now, don't get me wrong. The pure in heart getting to see God is certainly cool, but I'd rather inherit the earth or get mercy or comfort. What's so great about seeing God? I mean, technically, He's so holy that we can't even look on Him directly; the sight would vaporize us. Then I remembered something Jesus said: "Truly, I tell all of you with certainty, the Son can do nothing of His own accord, but only what He sees the Father doing. What the Father does, the Son does likewise" (John 5:19 ISV). By having a pure heart, we get to see what God the Father is doing. Like the popular saying, WWJD (What Would Jesus Do?), we can go and join in on the action.

When you combine these first four Ps, you have put on the full armor of God, which prepares you for every encounter. He will provide for all your needs when you have developed a sound travel plan that establishes your priority objective: seeking God's Kingdom and His righteousness first, which helps train your heart and mind to see life from His perspective. You've established your path by trusting in Him, which gives you confidence and peace of mind throughout your journey. This maximizes your potential so that God can use all of who you are for His purpose, and He strengthens your confidence so that you can "see" what the Father is doing. You can't be in a better place than knowing that you are right where the Father wants you.

The reward you will have in your heart is beyond comprehension when you are aligned with Him. "Delight yourself in the Lord, and He will give you the desires of your heart" (Psalm 37:4 ESV). That's such a cool promise that you had better keep your teeth brushed, as you'll have a perpetual grin on your face.

The final P brings it all together: it is the Process by which you travel. There are many verses that describe this, but the following two verses sum up both the breadth and depth of our motivation. The first is 1 Corinthians 16:14 (NIV): "Do everything in love." This shows that the breadth of our motivation should be all-encompassing. The second is John 15:12 (NASB): "This is My commandment, that you love one another, just as I have loved you." This shows the depth. Jesus, the Son of God, died for you. There is no greater example of selfless love than that. The Bible is a love story about the Creator and His constant pursuit of His beloved creation—humankind.

When asked what the greatest commandment was, Jesus replied that you must love the Lord your God with all your heart, mind, body, soul, and strength—once again, it's all you got, and then He added that we shall love our neighbors as ourselves (Matt. 22:36–39). Upon these two commands rest all the laws, rules, and regulations of the whole Bible, and it has only one verb: love. We love God in the vertical—He is above us—and we love our neighbors in the horizontal as our peers. When put together, this forms the shape of the cross, where God so loved the world that He gave His only begotten Son so that whoever believes in Him shall not perish, but have eternal life (John 3:16). It's an amazing love story.

We are tasked to carry this cross in our Christian journey. We are to pick up our cross daily and follow Christ (Luke 9:23). This cross is made out of love—loving God through our praise and worship of Him (the vertical beam) and by loving our neighbors through our unselfish acts of kindness and consideration (the horizontal beam). This is our "burden" or cross to bear such that we love our way through every situation and circumstance that we face. It requires sacrifice to consider others better than ourselves, to help those in need, to be humble, and even to love those who do not like us. This cross may make us a target for ridicule from those who mock God or from those who do not respect our adherence to ethical principles. It is a cross that can endanger a person's life in certain nations, but Jesus commands us to carry this cross of love.

In Paul's first letter to the Corinthians, he describes the importance of love as the vital ingredient in every action we take. The entire thirteenth chapter of 1 Corinthians is often referred to as the "love" chapter. In it, Paul states that even if we could talk to angels, and we did it without love, it would just be noise. If we knew everything about everything or had so much faith and power that we could move mountains, but we did it without love, it would be worth nothing. If we were to sacrifice our life, and it was not motivated by love, then it would be a total waste. Love is the key motivation for all action:

> Love is patient; love is kind and is not jealous; love does not brag and is not arrogant, does not act unbecomingly; it does not seek its own, is not provoked, does not take into account a wrong suffered, does not rejoice in unrighteousness, but rejoices with the truth; love bears all things, believes all things, hopes all things, endures all things. Love never fails (1 Cor. 13:4–8a NASB).

As I write this, I've come up with another "P". Although it is somewhat implied with the other Ps, it should be acknowledged separately because it is so important. This P is for Partner. In this journey through life, you are never alone. Jesus is always with you. He said it Himself: "I am with you always, even to the end of the age" (Matt. 28:20b NLT). He is the greatest travel partner you can have. Maybe I should add a seventh P to make it a perfect number: Proclamation. That's our job on this journey. To go forth and tell everyone you know how awesome it is to be a follower of Christ. We are to spread the Gospel News *and* make them disciples (or followers) of Jesus Christ. He is a wonderful Savior, a perfect travel companion, and the ultimate way to travel.

One final thought: You played sports enough, so you know that in order to improve yourself, you have to work at it consistently. You can't just jump in a pool and be an expert swimmer, or play a clarinet well without practice. Spiritual growth requires the same level of dedication. You have to work at it in a consistent manner, and it takes time to develop. It's a lifelong process. As disciples, which means we are students of Christ, we are always learning, and we never graduate in this lifetime. As stated earlier, we all have just one life to live, and we do not know how long we have. The clock is constantly ticking, and unfortunately, there are no time outs, nor is there a pause button that we can press. We are now closer to death than when you first started reading this book, and that applies to everyone; the irony of life and death is that as soon as we are born, we are simultaneously both living and dying.

Referring once again to consulting best practices, when solving a problem, you state the objective you want to achieve or where you want to be (Future State), you evaluate where you are (Current State), and then you determine the best way to get from where you are to where you want to be. In *The 7 Habits of Highly Successful People*, Stephen Covey states that the second habit is to "begin with the end in mind." Knowing where you want to end up helps you determine how to get there. Life's a journey best traveled with a destination in mind. Generically speaking, the objective in life is that everyone wants to be successful; it just depends on how each individual defines success.

In the final analysis, the only opinion that matters is God's, and therefore, we should be diligently focused on God's Kingdom both here on earth and in the life to come. At some point after this life on earth, we will all have to give an accounting for what we have done. "And inasmuch as it is appointed for men to die once and after this comes judgment" (Heb. 9:27 NASB). To succeed in this life is to stand before His Throne and hear God say to you, "Well done, good and faithful servant."

Actually, it may be even better than that. Those who have accepted Jesus Christ as their Lord and Savior have become adopted children of God and heirs to His Kingdom. Our Heavenly Father knows what is absolutely best for you, for your sister, for me, and for every person on the globe. He longs for a relationship with you and wants you to trust Him, not just for your needs, but to live a life that is full and fruitful. Our Heavenly Father wants to bless us, and He knows how. If given a choice between letting myself choose what is best for me and letting God choose what is best for me, who do you think will make the better decision? I think God will, and if you apply the same question to yourself, you will reach the same answer.

Paul tells us in the first couple of verses in chapter 12 of Romans that we are to offer ourselves as living sacrifices; we are not to be conformed to the world, but be transformed by the renewing of our minds in Christ Jesus. We must surrender our will and seek the will and direction from the Holy Spirit that dwells within us. I don't have all the answers here, as I have not even remotely mastered this part, because *surrendering*, *yielding*, and *sacrificing* are words that naturally do not appeal to me.

It's interesting that as you grow in faith, you notice a change in your prayer life. At first, we appeal to God as this cosmic genie: Please give us our desires. Then, as we mature, we begin to seek His Kingdom and think in terms of His Kingdom, and we pray for our Father to help us achieve goals that we think He wants us to achieve. This is a definite improvement, but it still has the concept of asking God what He will do for us. The final stage is achieving that sense of surrender and trust and knowing that God has your best interests at heart. Then your prayers to the Father will be more like, "What will You do through me?" It's okay to ask God whatever you wish. He tells us to do so. Even Jesus asked before His crucifixion if there was a Plan B, as He wasn't too excited about Plan A. Yet, He concluded with, "Not as I will, but as Thou wilt." Similarly, as we grow in faith, we continue to ask for anything, but we must "be prepared" to accept His answer and have the obedience to follow through with it.

As God's adopted son, you should earnestly seek His will on earth as it is in Heaven. By doing so, you will receive His blessings, guidance, and grace. Then, as one who has been truly faithful, you will hear God lovingly say to you on that final day, "This is my son with whom I am well pleased." That, dear nephew, is true success and a journey that was travelled well.

Stay safe and lots of love,
Your Uncle

40. A "Soul" Purpose

Lela Battistini

Sitting at my computer, controlling the urge to throw it across the room, I am interrupted once again. For starters, my computer is so slow that it could be going backwards. On top of that, every page I try to load says, "server not found." How can that be when I know I have an Internet connection? So I close out of Mozilla Firefox, let it rest for a minute, then pull it up again. It will work, but only for a short period of time. So I close out again, unplug it from the router and modem, and count to ten. I do this because the manual says to and because if you're angry, you're supposed to take a deep breath and count to ten. So this is what I did, several times over the previous couple of days. I am using a desktop, but I know it can be throwable.

As soon as I get it working and I think I'm on a roll, I get interrupted. My children are fighting or it's time to take them to Vacation Bible School or pick them up. I have to go clean a house, or the phone rings, or I have to change our Webelos camping trip plans, or somebody is hungry. The last straw for me tonight was having my son, who should have been in bed, come to me at the desk and ask me a question. Remember, I am already frustrated, angry and think there are way too many Scripture quotes in this book that I am working on.

I am the unofficial editor of this book before it goes to the real editor. I am referencing Bible quotes, to denote the translations used (NIV, NLT, etc.) as a writer cannot simply put book, chapter, and verse. I am also checking for spelling and grammatical errors and highlighting any changes. It is tedious, challenging, and time-consuming work. When the computer won't cooperate, it is maddening as well. I am to the point of giving up for the night, but I am on deadline...and then my nine-year-old son Casey appears at my side.

I turn to him and tell him to go to bed.

He says he has a question.

I say, "Fine, what is it?"

He replies to me in a nervous, swaying way, "What is sin?"

I gape at him. I wasn't expecting that. I thought it was a delay tactic to keep from going to bed. I have learned to just let my kids say what they've got to say, and then send them back to bed, instead of saying, "Go to bed." It eliminates a repeat performance of coming back and trying to ask whatever question they think is so important. But this one threw me for a loop.

The kids have been going to Vacation Bible School all week, so I asked him if this was what he was learning there.

He said, "Yes," so I pulled up the Ten Commandments through Google. I did not have trouble with loading that page. I read them to him one by one and tried to explain, in kid language, what each commandment meant. He then tried to interpret what I was saying by repeating it in his own words. I would correct him, and I definitely told him Transformers had *nothing* to do with it. Bumblebee and Optimus Prime weren't involved.

But in his mind, they might be. He asked, "When Optimus Prime said to Bumblebee that one of the Transformers shouldn't die in vain, was that what one of the commandments meant?"

Well, sorta. I explained that *in vain* meant *for no purpose.* "To use God's name in vain," I said, "means to use it for anything other than praising Him."

Whew. We made it past the Ten Commandments. He then told me he was playing the angel in the burning furnace.

I said, "There is no burning furnace." Okay, duh me. I was thinking modern technology, not biblical times. They didn't have home furnaces back then.

He kissed me goodnight and walked away.

Lo and behold, the next story I started editing, as soon as he walked away, was the story of Shadrach, Meshach, and Abednego. I didn't fall out of my chair, but it was close. I called him back into the room, and I said all those names and the king's.

He said, "I can't pronounce their names, but that is the story."

I said, "You get to play God's angel in the fire?"

He said yes. So I read him the story.

By golly, it said "furnace." We went back to the Ten Commandments where the one says do not worship statues and false gods. I explained that this is what God was talking about. The king was so important to himself that he had a statue made, and he wanted everyone to bow before it. Those three guys said, "No," because they would only worship the one true God, so they were thrown into the furnace. However, an angel of God walked with them and protected them.

I told him there is only one God and only one Jesus, and that if He lives in our hearts we are saved. I told him God is everywhere, and when he began looking around the room for God, I explained that He was invisible.

He asked me where everywhere was, so I said, "In our hearts."

Casey told me he wanted to go to Heaven by going to where Jesus died and climb the bridge to shake hands with God. (Not sure where this came from.) He asked where Jesus had died, and I told him Jesus died in Jerusalem. I told him there is no literal bridge to Heaven, and the only way to get there is to believe that Jesus is the Son of God. You should live your life making God happy and when you die, God welcomes you into Heaven.

Now, tell me God doesn't work in mysterious ways? I haven't had any problems with my computer since then, either.

I told Tom (the creator of *Short Strolls in Faith*) that I didn't have any stories to share to include in this book. I didn't want to think of any, and some things I just don't want to remember but my son Casey opened my eyes with his childlike wonder of all that is holy and just. We should all seek Him with such innocence. It reminds us that we adults need to do more than brush up on our Scripture to answer questions during Vacation Bible School. We need to incorporate Scripture into our daily lives—myself included. I recognize the fact that I am doing this for a reason. Even though I have obstacles impeding my progress, somebody, somewhere is learning the Word of God. Tonight it was me, through my son's innocent question and his "soul" purpose for still being awake.

41. God with Us!

Tom McAllister

There is something exciting about the start of a new year. It's really just another day, not much different from the previous day, but there's something about the prospect of a new beginning that produces a new and refreshing hope for the future. Many people make resolutions on what to improve in their lives. A new year allows for self-reflection. It is a time to pause and evaluate priorities and one's perspective on life. It is an opportunity to redefine what is important.

If we contemplate the Christmas season, it parallels this sentiment. It's a new birth—the birth of our Lord and Savior, Christ Jesus. The prophet Isaiah predicted His birth seven hundred years before He was born. In Isaiah 7:14 (NLT), the prophet wrote, "The Lord Himself will give you the sign. Look! The virgin will conceive a child! She will give birth to a son and will call Him Immanuel [which means 'God is with us']."

Immanuel—God with us. What a comforting thought. As the apostle John describes in his Gospel, the Word became flesh in Christ and dwelt among us. Jesus, the Word of God, was born humbly in a manger, fully human, and yet, mysteriously, fully God—God with us.

Do you have Jesus with you today? Do you have Him in your heart?

If not, then *why not?* Choosing to let Jesus dwell within us is the most important decision that you will ever make.

Let's stop to contemplate the available options and alternatives. *Hmmm, let's see....*we have as one choice the Creator of this incredibly massive universe that contains over a hundred billion billion stars, and He knows each one by name, He knows the number of hairs on my head and on the heads of all living creatures. He knows all things and is more powerful than everything else put together. He loves me and wants what is best for me, and He *knows* what is best for me. He desires an intimate, personal relationship with me, and all I have to do is respond to Him, accept Him, and love Him. Or I can forsake all that and do my own thing. I can Sinatra it and do it my way, or modify the Nike slogan and "Just wing it." It's amazing how many people choose the latter, or else they fail to fully embrace the former. Perhaps it's a commitment thing.

Think about this for a moment. What would life be like having Jesus with you every day? Let's consider an important day. It's also a very happy day. Ladies, what's a very important day for you? I'm not talking about the day after Thanksgiving when everything is on sale and you spend the day in a perpetual, heart-palpitating frenzy ensuring that no bargain is left unconsidered. Take a moment to think of one of the most momentous days in your lifetime.

Yes, we're speaking of your wedding day. Granted, it is a very important day for the bride and the groom, but I think it is more special to the bride. It is a day in which you want everything to go perfectly. It is also, like a new year, a new start of a new life together with that special someone you are joining your life with in marriage. Today, many people have very sophisticated weddings, and they require a lot of planning and organizing. Not only are there a multitude of tasks to be performed to prepare for the big day, but the wedding itself requires a significant amount of choreography of filming, photos, catering, and the like. For many couples, trying to coordinate all the wedding activities can cause a lot of stress and worry, as managing the event is almost a full-time job. One solution is to hire a wedding planner and thus delegate all the detailed planning and logistics to someone else. So if you were getting married and had the opportunity to hire a wedding planner, who would you choose? What if you could choose Jesus to be your wedding planner? Do you think He would be a good choice?

Do you think you would have to worry about whether the wedding activities would be a success? I think you would sleep very soundly, for you would not have to worry about anything. What could go wrong with Jesus as your wedding planner?

Consider some of the many problems that Jesus could solve:

The bar has run out of alcohol, and all we have left is water. Jesus turned water into wine, and at a wedding no less, so He's done this one before, and He could easily turn water into whatever favorite beverage your taste buds desire.

Oh no! The caterers' refrigeration unit is broken, and all the food is spoiled. All we have left is five bags of chips and a pint of salsa! Go tell Jesus—He fed five thousand with two fishes and five loaves of bread.

The power has gone out in the church, and we have no lights. Jesus can handle it. He simply spoke, "Let there be light," and light came into being across the whole universe. He already is the light of the world.

Look! There's a storm coming, and the wind is blowing, and it's going to rain and ruin our outdoor wedding. Just tell Jesus—He'll tell the storm to stop, and all will become calm.

The groom's got cold feet! Jesus will wash his feet and warm his heart to give him confidence in his life ahead with his new bride.

As you see, Jesus could solve any problem if He was your wedding planner. Everything would go as planned, and you would have peace of mind that everything would be fine. So wouldn't it be great to have Jesus as your wedding planner? Well, if you would want Jesus to be with you on your one special day—your wedding day—why wouldn't you want Him with you every day?

That makes sense, doesn't it? If you want Jesus with you on important days, then it seems logical to have Him with you every day. The great news is that He wants to be with you.

God desires a relationship with each and every one of us, but He doesn't want a distant relationship where we just check in periodically or have Him on speed-dial in case of an emergency. He wants a close relationship with us. Jesus gave us an illustration of what He desires.

"Behold, I stand at the door and knock; if anyone hears My voice and opens the door, I will come in to him and will dine with him, and he with Me" (Rev. 3:20 NASB).

So Jesus wants to come over for dinner, huh? What's the big deal about that? Well, dining can be a very intimate experience. That was even truer two thousand years ago. People were very concerned with having their next meal. There was no refrigeration, so planning for a meal was a daily event. They didn't have the convenience of twenty-four-hour Waffle Houses where you can get your hash browns scattered, smothered, chunked, or chopped. A meal was an important event, and to sit down and dine with someone was a very close and personal experience.

It still can be today. Have you been to a nice romantic setting with your spouse, significant other, or even just a close friend at an elegant restaurant that sets the proper mood so you can share your personal thoughts, ideas, goals, and desires?

God wants that level of intimacy with you.

However, in today's rat race, where cell phones and laptops are natural appendages to our bodies, and our quality of life seems to be measured by the number of events on our personal calendars, it's hard to find time for such an intimate experience. At best, we may be able to squeeze in a dinner with the Lord at a drive-thru. "Hey, Jesus, you want fries with that?"

If your life is that way, then you're missing out on everything but the indigestion. God is love—the most wonderful love you can ever imagine. Our Lord knows what issues you face and what challenges you have. He can mentor you through any situation, and He does so with incredible compassion and mercy. He has the best game plan for your life. We are created in His image, and a part of our being in His image is our ability to love and our ability to choose whom to love. So God doesn't just want to hear from you on important days or when you are in trouble; walk with Him and talk with Him, and share with Him all of your life each day. In the Gospel of John, verse 15:15, Jesus called His disciples "His friends." We too are His friends, and His love and friendship are the greatest treasure a person can have.

Now some of you may be thinking, "Okay. That's all well and good; to have Jesus on the good days or even the average days is a worthwhile endeavor, but what about the sad days? If Jesus is supposedly with me, then where is He or what is He doing when I lose my job? Where is Jesus when tragedy hits? When a storm destroys my house, when a family member finds out they have cancer, or when I discover my child is addicted to drugs—where is Jesus then? When those things happen, why isn't He doing something about it?"

When the going gets tough, why does it appear that Jesus gets going?

There's a story in the Bible in the book of John, chapter 11, that you may be familiar with: the story about Lazarus. Along with his two sisters, Mary and Martha, Lazarus was Jesus's close friend. Jesus had left Judea because the Jews wanted to kill Him, so He crossed the Jordan River where John the Baptist had been baptizing people, and He and His disciples were staying there. Lazarus became very sick, and his sisters sent word to Jesus to come. Yet Jesus stayed where He was for two more days. Jesus, like a grandmaster chess champion, knew what was about to happen. He was thinking several moves ahead. He knew it was part of God's plan to perform an incredible miracle of raising Lazarus from the dead as a foreshadowing of His own upcoming death and resurrection. So He told His disciples, "Let us go back to Judea." His disciples were stunned. They objected, advising Him that it was not a good idea, as the last time they were there, the Pharisees tried to kill Him. But Jesus told them that Lazarus was dead.

So Jesus already knows that Lazarus is dead, and when He returns to Bethany, which is a small town outside of Jerusalem, He is greeted by Martha, Lazarus's sister, who comes out to meet Jesus just outside the city limits. Martha is crying. She says, "Oh Jesus, if you had only been here, then my brother would not have died." She leaves and tells her sister Mary, and then Mary gets up and goes to see Jesus.

Lazarus had many friends, and they all were there mourning in support of his two sisters, so when Mary got up to go see Jesus, many of the people followed her, as they thought she was going to the gravesite to weep there. That is where Jesus meets Mary, and with her is a huge crowd of people, and everyone is crying and wailing. It is truly a very sad and emotional scene.

Jesus knows that He is going to revive Lazarus and raise him from the dead as a testimony to His power over death as the true Son of God. So He knows what He is going to do, but what does He do first?

He *doesn't* say, "All right, everyone, just calm down! I'm Jesus, and I'm going to fix everything, so quit your crying." No, He doesn't do that at all. Jesus pauses for a moment to embrace their grief, and He has compassion for their circumstances. It's the shortest verse in the Bible, yet one of the most powerful: "Jesus wept" (John 11:35 NASB).

Jesus Christ, the Son of God, the One through Whom all things were created both by Him and for Him (John 1:3 and Col. 1:16); the One Whom every knee will bow and tongue confess as Lord; the One Who already knows that He is going to resolve this particular dilemma, pauses for a moment in His compassion for us. He gets down in the trenches of our pain and suffering and weeps right alongside of us. Now is that an awesome Savior or what?

The Son of God, Who sits at the right hand of God the Father Almighty, is so concerned about you and your well-being that He will get beside you in your worst moments and grieve with you. Wow!

For those of you who know the rest of the story, Jesus went to the tomb of Lazarus, had them roll away the stone in front of the tomb, and with a loud voice, He commanded, "Lazarus, come out!" And Lazarus did. He was all wrapped up in burial linens, and Jesus said, "Unbind him and turn him loose." Sadness and grief were turned into joy! And many people there who witnessed this believed in Him.

If that's not sufficiently inspiring, consider what transpired the following week. Jesus, the King of kings and Lord of lords, allowed Himself to be arrested, tortured, and crucified for us on a cross. He died in place of us so that we might share a life with Him for all eternity—what an incredible sacrificial act of love. We have done nothing to justify this amazing act of mercy. In fact, it is just the opposite: God so loves us that "while we were yet sinners, Christ died for us" (Rom. 5:8).

So do you believe in Him? To accept Christ as your Lord and Savior is the most important decision you can make, and it is the greatest thing that you can do. Salvation does not depend on what you do, but whom you know and trust, and there is nothing more important in all of life than for you to know and trust Jesus Christ as your Lord. If He was willing to die for you, shouldn't you be willing to live for Him? Think of the reverse: What profit or gain is there if you were to rule the whole world—to be the wealthiest, most famous, most respected and desired person in the world—and yet lose your soul? It would be a total loss. So don't wait. Now is your chance. Accept Him as Lord.

If you have Christ as your Savior, then make your resolution this year to draw closer to Him. Focus on building your relationship with Him through reading His Word and being conscious of His presence. It's great to have Him with you on the happy days, the regular days, and most importantly, on the sad days. He will celebrate with you in your victories, be a friend and counselor in your daily routine, and be your comforter in times of grief. He promises that He will never leave you or forsake you, even unto the end of time.

Now having Jesus with you does not guarantee a life of ease. A quick look at the lives of the disciples will tell you that. Life can be harsh at times, and we will all be tested and suffer through trials—some of us more than others. Picking up your cross each day and following Christ can bring hardship, suffering, ridicule, and in some cases, death.

The world will not be made right until Christ sets up the New Jerusalem—His Kingdom here on earth. Then there will be no more pain and no more tears. Until then, we must persevere and look forward to the final hope of glory. The best way to do that is to have Jesus with you every step of the way. Take Him into your heart and dine with Him. There is no greater food and no better company.

42. The Shining

Tom McAllister

And God said, "Let there be

$$\nabla \cdot \mathbf{E} = \rho/\varepsilon_0$$
$$\nabla \cdot \mathbf{B} = 0$$
$$\nabla \times \mathbf{E} = -\partial \mathbf{B}/\partial t$$
$$\nabla \times \mathbf{B} = \mu_0 \mathbf{J} + \mu_0 \varepsilon_0 (\partial \mathbf{E}/\partial t)$$

And there was light" (Gen. 1:3 NSB [Nerdy Science Bible]).[1]

Okay, a little geek humor—just thought you might get a charge out of it. The above are Maxwell's equations describing electromagnetic radiation or light. God is the omniscient Scientist. He is the original Author and Inventor of all creation. Human scientists can mathematically calculate how the laws work, but God created the laws in the first place. We should never make "light" of that fact.

We should however, be a light. Jesus said, "Let your light shine before men in such a way that they may see your good works, and glorify your Father who is in Heaven" (Matt. 5:16 NASB).

So let's break this divine directive down into its component parts. Our first requirement is to let our light shine. You can't have a light without a light source, and we can't shine without God. He spoke light into existence and He is the Source of all light—physical, intellectual, and spiritual.

This God-sourced light of ours is to shine before men or before all people. This means that we are to be an example to others. How? By having others see our good works. The best form of leadership is to lead by example. The best testimony is through your actions. Talk is cheap. When you walk the walk, your walk will talk the talk.

These works that we do are not just any works, but good works. As Jesus said, "Only God is truly good" (Luke 18:19b NLT). Therefore, these works must be those inspired by God to accomplish His will. Our role in this world is to submit to God and make ourselves available for His purpose to do His bidding. In a sense, we are all tools in God's toolkit, so when He reaches for us, we should not be stuck in our strap holder or hiding out down in the bottom of His bag. When we have surrendered our spirit to God's will, then we are ready for His use in accordance with His plan and we will produce good works.

One of the key parts of this verse is contained in the prepositional phrase, "in such a way." Our light is to shine in a particular manner. What is this manner or way? It is to be a blessing to others. The good works that we do should benefit our fellow man. We are to love one another as Christ loved us. The Greek word for this kind of love is *agape*. It is a selfless love—a love without judgment or a love provided without it being merited. We just give it. The King James Bible refers to this type of love as *charity*. Life is already tough, and we all have needs, so we should give of ourselves and help out one another through gentle words of encouragement and generous acts of kindness. Doing unto others as you would want done unto you is not complicated. It's not Maxwell's equations. Just do it.

A friend once loaned me a book to read. It was somewhat New Age so I wasn't too impressed overall, but the author coined a really neat word and it should be in the English language. We should strive to be *loveful*. We can be *thoughtful, mindful,* and *thankful,* but it would be best if we all were *loveful*. We should live our lives full of love. If the people of this world behaved in such a way, there would be so much light on this earth that we would not have an energy crisis.

Finally, what is the ultimate purpose for being a good example through our works of being loveful and a blessing to others? It is to give glory to God. He is our *raison d'etre*—our reason for being. He is our Creator and Lord. We give Him glory when we are used by Him for His purpose. Those who see our light will then recognize its source and give Him glory as well. It's a beautiful thing, and it is often contagious. Our light is a beacon of love. When we turn our light on, it will radiate in such a way that when others see the attitude that we have in the works that we do, they will declare in amazement, *that's a God thing!* Jesus forecasted this result of being *loveful* during the Last Supper when He said, "By this everyone will know that you are My disciples, if you love one another" (John 13:35 NIV).

As you near the end of this book, we hope it has provided some light to you. Since there were several contributors to this book, we chose to publish it under the collective pen name, B.A. Brightlight.

Who is B.A. Brightlight? B.A. Brightlight is you. It's me. It is all who have accepted Christ as Savior. It is preachers, clergy, Bible scholars, and blue-collar faith-walkers. Our mission is to share our light through our love to others—to be a blessing to all we meet. It is the living fulfillment of Matthew 25:34-40 where Jesus proclaimed that whenever you feed the poor, aid the sick, clothe the naked, and visit those in prison (even the least of these brothers of Mine), you did it to Me. This is being a bright light for the Lord. It is not for our glory, but for the glory of the Source of all light. It is for the glory of God.

Now it's time for us to light it up. The whole world is in a crisis, and our nation has very serious challenges ahead. America has always been a light to others. We have always been that shining city on the hill. It's now time that we citizens fix our electrical short and get US beaming again. Like most electrical applications, we need to be properly grounded. The only way to be properly grounded is to be grounded in Christ. Jesus is the light of the world, and we bask in His light. Through His in-dwelt Spirit in us, we should radiate His glow. That's one of our mission statements. So go out, crank up the wattage, serve and love others such that you give them a Son-tan.

Let's all be a bright light for the LORD!

Epilogue

Although our short stroll is now over, the journey continues. I hope you have received blessings and refreshment in our brief encounter and that you now have a few spiritual nuggets to carry with you in your upcoming travels. It has been our pleasure to share our thoughts and stories and we wish you Godspeed and His blessings in all your future endeavors for there is much more work to be done.

As the apostle Paul tells us, "For our battle is not against flesh and blood, but against the rulers, against the authorities, against the world powers of this darkness, against the spiritual forces of evil in the heavens" (Eph. 6:12 HCS). It is a war out there! It's a war that far too many people are losing of which the vast majority of them aren't even aware that they are in a fight. Imagine that! They are engulfed in a war over the most precious thing they have—their soul—and they are oblivious to the battle. Talk about being unarmed! So we need to arm them with the truth. That Truth is a Person. That Truth is Jesus Christ.

Yes, Satan is a defeated foe. He has been judged and is awaiting the execution of his sentence which will ultimately confine him to an eternity in the lake of fire. Meanwhile, he is still prince of this world and he constantly fills the earth with his lies and deceit. We witness its grotesqueness in the lust of power among leaders who kill and commit atrocities against their own people in their attempt to remain in control. We see its subtleties in the whisper to pursue carnal desires—if it feels good, do it, if no one sees it, then who cares, if it gives me an advantage at the expense of others, then go for it. And of course the worst lie of all—there is no God, so have a great time—which is two lies in one.

It's time to put a stop to the lies.

Though we cannot prevent Satan from telling them, we can arm and equip others to recognize the lies and not fall into their snare. We can counter the deceit by promoting the truth and the slap, dadgum awesomeness of following Jesus Christ! We serve a great God! He loves us, has a plan of prosperity for us, and will guide us in our journey to the most excellent life ever! So let's get out there and share this Great News! Let's retrieve the lost from darkness to light. Let's encourage our fellow believers and help them when they stumble or waiver in their faith.

Rick Saltzer poignantly revealed to us in chapter one, "Don't waste time" so let's get after it, go all in, put on the full armor of God, pick up our cross of love and follow Christ, praying unceasingly as we go. There are literally billions of opportunities out there. It's a target rich environment—a salesman's dream and we have the greatest product in the universe: everlasting love and eternal life. You can go overseas, but there is plenty of action here in the U.S. Our nation is spiritually flailing in search of truth and we seem to be looking for love in all the wrong places. We certainly need to pray for our leaders, but if we truly want real hope and positive change, it must start with us—we the people.

As stated before and it needs repeating until it is emblazoned in our hearts and minds, "If we the people, who are called by His name, will humble ourselves, repent of our wicked ways, seek His face and go to the LORD in prayer, He will hear our prayer, forgive our sins, and heal our land." This is our solution!

It starts with you and it starts with me and it grows to we—we the people. May we the people through His amazing grace unite in heart, mind, body, and soul and be a bright light for the Lord. If we do this, it will be an awesome thing to see. Let's follow Him on *the* most excellent journey of our lives. Let's make it happen. Let us start today!

Endnotes

CHAPTER 4

1. *Holman Quick Source Guide to Christian Apologetics*, Doug Powell, p252–255.

CHAPTER 10

1. en.wikipedia.org/wiki/Arthur Andersen
2. Ibid.

CHAPTER 18

1. U.S. Constitution, Article VII, p 4, quote: "done in Convention by the Unanimous Consent of the States present the Seventeenth Day of September in the Year of our Lord one thousand seven hundred and Eighty seven..."

CHAPTER 21

1. *Israel My Glory* magazine: Jan/Feb 2010 "The Kingdom of the Beast" pp 22 Charles E. McCracken
2. *Israel My Glory* magazine: Jan/Feb 2010 "The Emergent Kingdom" pp 27–28 Gary Gilley
3. Ibid. Gilley p 27

CHAPTER 28

1. Much insight for this article came from Hal Lindsey's much-recommended, comprehensive review of the Gospel of John.

CHAPTER 30

1. Holman Quick Source Guide to Christian Apologetics, Doug Powell, p 39–41.

CHAPTER 42

1. http://scienceblogs.com/builtonfacts/2009/08/ maxwells_equations _light.php

Bible Translation Abbreviations

New International Version   (NIV)
New Living Translation   (NLT)
English Standard Version   (ESV)
New American Standard Bible   (NASB)
International Standard Version   (ISV)
GOD'S WORD Translation   (GWT)
King James Bible   (KJB)
American King James Bible   (AKJB)
American Standard Version   (ASV)
Darby Bible Translation   (DBT)
English Revised Version   (ERV)
Holman Christian Standard   (HCS)
Webster's Bible Translation   (WBT)
Young's Literal Translation   (YLT)
The Message   (MSG)

NOTE: Scripture verses used in this book were referenced from the website: www.biblos.com. Any denotation of a scripture verse that does not have a specific translation is for the reader's reference only. It is a partial verse or has combined verbiage from more than one translation.

Acknowledgements

A special thanks to all the "blue collar" contributing authors:

Lela Battistini lives in Sharpsburg, Georgia and is the proud mother of five children. She owns "Free at Last" Cleaning Services and provided significant editing work in the writing of this book.

Chance Castleberry is the co-founder and president of Turning Point Recovery Resources. He lives in Gainesville, Georgia with his wife and two children.

Marcia Daniels is a retired Air Force major, inspirational speaker, writer, and distributor for Reliv products. She lives in Oklahoma City, OK and is a member of Bethlehem Star Baptist church where she serves as Director of Little Star School, nursery, and puppet programs.

Doug Hanson is a retired executive from The DuPont Company. Originally, from Texas where he met and married Lynne, his wife of 49 years, they have three children and nine grandchildren. He leads and participates in mission work and is a member of First Baptist church in Gainesville.

Emmett Holley lives in Gainesville, GA with his wife Ellen and his son and daughter. Disabled due to his battle with cancer, he still does motivational speaking for churches and non-profit organizations. He is a former deacon at First Baptist church in Gainesville.

Jeff McAdams was saved by the grace of God at the age of 30. His professional career has been in retail management since graduating from Appalachian State University in 1983. He is unmarried and lives in Graham, NC where he attends Graham Presbyterian church.

Kathryn Rogers is a mother and a wife. Desiring to make a difference in another's life, she was led by the Lord to become a Stephen Minister Leader. She and her husband live in St Louis, MO and are members of Kirkwood Baptist church.

Rick Saltzer is employed as a healthcare representative in central Pennsylvania where he lives with his wife and two sons.

Zoraya Valdez lives in Gainesville, GA with her son, Eliseo. She owns and operates a lawn care and landscaping company. She recently served as interim minister for a start-up Hispanic ministry in Roswell, GA. She was ordained as a minister (transitioned from "blue collar" to "white collar") in 2011.

Jack Wehmiller and his wife C.J. live in Murrayville, GA. They have two sons and five grandchildren. They have served in various positions while members of First Baptist church in Gainesville for 23 years. Retired from the sales and marketing industry, Jack and C.J. are commissioned "field personnel" with the Cooperative Baptist Fellowship and Jack also works with Rivers of the World ministry.

Also, special thanks, in loving memory, for her efforts of editorial assistance to **Crystal Downs** who has since been promoted to heaven.

From family members, friends, insightful teachers and leaders, there are far too many people to list in thanks for their contribution of inspiration and support for the writing of this book. However, there are three people that I want to single out. One is my Mom who read through multiple versions of each story and provided her loving encouragement and wise insight into each reading. The second is my Dad, who never got to read this, but his consistent love, patience, and grace through my many prodigal son adventures was so inspiringly Christlike to me. And finally to my great friend and fellow author Emmett Holley whose walk through the long and deep valley of cancer with a smile on his face and joy in his heart to share encouragement and the love of Christ to others has been such a very, very bright light for me and for many.

In our Christian walk, we are all out there casting seeds, adding water, pulling weeds, tilling the ground, and assisting with the harvest. The individuals that we meet in our journey through life all contribute to our final mosaic piece of art that defines who we are. The greatest contributor and True Source, of course, is Christ. Amen.

We welcome your comments! If you have any comments or a story or testimony that you want to share, then please email us at: BCF@BABRIGHTLIGHT.COM.

Part of the proceeds gained through the sale of this book is donated to Growth Ministries International (www.gogmi.org). Growth Ministries International is a non-profit consulting company committed to serving and assisting churches and faith-based organizations grow and improve the efficiency and effectiveness of their ministry though the use of technology and best practice operational techniques.

Several of the stories in this book were originally presented in a book entitled, *Blue Collar Faith*, printed through CreateSpace publishing, 2011.